How to Spot

Butterflies

The How-to-Spot Series

How to Spot Butterflies, by Patricia Taylor Sutton and Clay Sutton
How to Spot Hawks & Eagles, by Clay Sutton and Patricia Taylor Sutton
How to Spot An Owl, by Patricia and Clay Sutton
How to Spot A Fox, by J. David Henry

How to Spot
Butterflies

Patricia Taylor Sutton
and Clay Sutton

PHOTOGRAPHY BY
PATRICIA TAYLOR SUTTON AND CLAY SUTTON

HOUGHTON MIFFLIN COMPANY
BOSTON

For information about permission to reproduce selections from this book, write to Permissions, Houghton Mifflin Company, 215 Park Avenue South, New York, NY 10003.

Library of Congress Cataloging-in-Publication Data

Sutton, Patricia, date.
    How to spot butterflies / Patricia Taylor Sutton and Clay Sutton.
      p. cm. -- (How to spot series)
    Includes bibliographical references and index.
    ISBN 0-395-89275-9
    1. Butterflies—North America. 2. Butterfly watching—North America.
I. Sutton, Clay, 1949- . II. Title. III. Series.
    QL548.S95 1999
    595.78'9'097--dc21   98-44701
                                 CIP

Designed by Susan McClellan

Quote on page 44 from *Handbook for Butterfly Watchers* © 1992 by Robert Michael Pyle. Reprinted by permission of Houghton Mifflin Company.

Poetry on page 69 from "Two Tramps in Mud Time" from *The Poetry of Robert Frost* edited by Edward Connery Lathem. Copyright 1936 by Robert Frost, © 1964 by Lesley Frost Ballantine, © 1969 by Henry Holt & Company. Reprinted by permission of Henry Holt and Company, Inc.

All photos by Patricia and Clay Sutton except the following:
Thea Pyle: 52
Jane Ruffin: 12, 14 bottom, 20, 22 top six, 27, 29 top, 31 bottom, 42, 75, 91, 102, 123, 138
    top middle, right second and third down, bottom middle, left bottom three
Ann Swengel: 92, 132
Dave Ward: 126

Contents

All common names used for butterflies are in accordance with the North American Butterfly Association's *Checklist & English Names of North American Butterflies* (1995).

Acknowledgments

WE'VE LEARNED SO MUCH from so many while afield in search of butterflies, whether for the simple pleasure of butterfly watching or while traveling, tagging, counting, photographing, gardening, or visiting gardens. Our thanks go out to all of you: Jane and Bill Ruffin, Wendy and Dennis Allen, Sheri Williamson and Tom Wood, Jim and Deb Dowdell, Robert Michael Pyle, the late Roger Tory Peterson, Jeff Glassberg and Jane Scott, Andrés Sada, Harry Darrow, Kenn Kaufman, Jim Brock, Ann and Scott Swengel, Denise Gibbs, Dave Ward, Vince Elia, Bob Barber, Jack and Jesse Connor, Louise Zemaitis, Karen Williams, Sandy Sherman, Bonnie Smith, Shawneen Finnegan, Joe and Sandy Usewicz, Liz Johnson, Dale Rosselet, Dave Sibley and Joan Walsh, Dale Schweitzer, Freddy Arthur, Billy McCord, Harry LeGrand, Barb Barton, Elizabeth Hunter, Gayle Steffy, Larissa Smith, Dick Walton, Dale and Jim Watson, Bob Dittrick and Lisa Moorehead, Pete and Linda Dunne, Mildred Morgan, Tony Leukering, Rick Radis, Jon Sutton, Judy Fieth and Michael Male.

It is always tough to single out individuals when the road to knowledge has been so long and winding, but a few have been special mentors. Special thanks to David Wright, who shared so much of his knowledge with each of our questions. His Cape May County butterfly checklist caught the birding community's attention and opened up another world of challenges and discoveries. Thanks to Jeff Glassberg for his field guides and for efforts to bring butterfly watchers across North America together through NABA. To Jim Dowdell, for whom all natural history is his quest, thanks for time afield together, companionship, skipper identification help, and teaching us how and where to look for the more elusive species. Special thanks to Bill Calvert for reviewing the Monarch section and for clarifying key points.

To three close friends who are always ready to head out for butterflies, no matter what. To Wendy Allen for always sharing her favorite South Carolina haunts with us — we've learned so much together. To Sheri Williamson, who came into our lives like a whirlwind, for shared travels through Arizona, Texas, and Alaska, and for teaching us so much about birds, bugs, and butterflies. Thanks for your "western review" of our manuscript. To Jane Ruffin, who has been a mentor from the first day we met, sharing a wealth of knowledge, books, contacts, and a zeal for Lepidoptera and butterfly watching, photography, and gardening.

Pat thanks the staff and board of the New Jersey Audubon Society for their understanding and support during this project. Last but far from least, we thank Pat's parents, Mary and George Taylor, and her family for their love and support, example and guidance. Finally, we thank Bill Bailey, our natural history mentor, for pulling us back from the big and showy displays of nature and exposing us to the tiny and easily overlooked wonders, such as hairstreaks, tiny weeds in bloom, and more!

Foreword

BY JEFFREY GLASSBERG, AUTHOR OF *Butterflies Through Binoculars* AND FOUNDER OF THE NORTH AMERICAN BUTTERFLY ASSOCIATION

WHEN PEOPLE LEARN that I am involved with butterflies, often the first thing they ask me is "I always used to see butterflies when I was a kid — how come there aren't any butterflies around anymore?" Part of the answer is that there really are fewer butterflies, especially in areas where there is little left in the way of natural vegetation, which, of course, is where most people live. But, another reason why you may see fewer butterflies now than when you were a child has to do with the way you live your life and the way in which you view the world. When you were a child you were small, observant, close to the ground, and probably played outside in fields of flowers — butterflies were a part of your world. Now, you're much larger than butterflies, may not pay much attention to the natural world, and probably don't spend so much of your time rolling in meadows! You've "outgrown" butterflies.

That's a shame because butterflies are little gems that reward close inspection with dazzling color, intricate patterns, and fascinating behavior. Spotting a butterfly may reawaken the excitement and delight you felt as a child — discovering the beauty and the fragility of the complex life swirling around you — and lead you to new adventures.

I can think of no better guides on this journey into the heart of the natural world than Pat and Clay Sutton. Having known Pat and Clay for more than six years, I can report that their enthusiasm is electrifying and that their knowledge is vast. In this welcome new book they introduce you to all the materials you will want on your journey, and they do so in a personable, highly readable fashion. After reading this book, you will see butterflies where before you saw none, and those which you had previously noticed, you will see in a new light.

I do have one caution for you. Once you spot your first Red-spotted Purple you may feel the need to spot a Pipevine Swallowtail. Before you know it you'll be searching for Striped Hairstreaks and Confused Cloudywings — you'll be hooked! Yes, butterflying is addictive, and this book is part of a small conspiracy to create as large a constituency as possible that cares deeply about the ecological health of the planet. Who knows, if we can save butterflies, we may even be able to save ourselves.

Preface

ENJOYING BUTTERFLIES BEYOND a casual level has long been almost completely the fief of the entomologist with a net. To study butterflies often meant netting, examining, and collecting them.

So much has changed in the past decade. Modern, close-focus binoculars enable close observation and enjoyment of live butterflies in the field. New field guides are being illustrated with live butterflies in natural settings, rather than dead, flat specimens.

Butterfly watching is steadily replacing butterfly collecting, in much the way that bird watching replaced bird shooting in the 1930s. Today, thousands of naturalists are truly "working without a net" and making major new contributions to our knowledge of butterfly status, distribution, behavior, and migration.

There are many obvious conservation spin-offs. Rare or uncommon butterflies can absorb a lot more watching than they can collecting. Too, as the hobby grows, the rapidly growing base of butterfly knowledge can go a long way toward identifying and protecting dwindling habitats. Many butterfly species all over our nation are threatened, some seriously, from a variety of causes, including pesticides, herbicides, pollution, traffic, mowing, and modern farming practices. Mainly, however, butterflies are threatened today by habitat loss and habitat degradation. In much of the country, the classic fallow "old field" weedy habitat is becoming increasingly hard to find. The won-derful part about butterfly watching is that you are not adding to the problem. Indeed, your observations and finds may even lead to additional protection.

It has amazed us how quickly this revolution is occurring. The North American Butterfly Association (NABA), founded in 1992, had grown to 3,000 members after only six years. It is heartening to see how many birders have embraced butterfly watching. We'll never forget an encounter with birders about ten years ago in the Canadian Rockies. While we were watching butterflies in a roadside mountain meadow, a car pulled up and a group of four jumped out as one. "What have you got? Rosy-Finches?" "No," we replied, "we're looking at a Common Alpine." "A what?" came the reply, the confusion flickering behind the bird patches indicating that momentarily, at least, he thought that he had missed that one in his bird guide. As they realized that we were looking at butterflies, a disdainful sigh indicated that we should feel guilty for waylaying them in their bird search. They squealed their tires pulling away.

Today, ten years later, many birders share an intense interest in butterflies. This burgeoning interest is particularly heartening in light of the fact that invertebrates have so long been ignored in inventory, survey, and protection efforts. It is satisfying to see the confusion or indifference of ten years ago likely replaced today with interest, or even fascination, by fellow naturalists and birders.

We are still avid birders, and always will be, but are continually reminded of how well birding and butterflying go hand in hand. Great birding spots are invariably good butterfly-watching spots as well and vice versa. We have thrilled to the Red Warblers at the winter Monarch roost in Mexico and been torn between watching Swallow-tailed Kites overhead or Atalas in the palmetto patches of the Florida Everglades. If you are a birder already, you will be amazed how butterfly watching can push all the same buttons. Finding butterflies and solving identification challenges is remarkably similar to finding and identifying birds. Separating skippers may be just the thing for you if you love the challenge of confusing fall warblers. And if you are not coming to butterflies from a birding background, you can still thrill to the subtle beauty and details of butterflies through close-focus binoculars.

Butterflies can be enjoyed almost everywhere in North America, from Kansas prairies to Arctic tundra, from the Sonoran Desert to a New Jersey barrier beach. When you become aware of butterflies you will notice and enjoy them in such unlikely times and places as a crisp October afternoon in New York City's Central Park or on sweltering August mornings in Tucson's desert heat.

Because of their fascinating life cycles, butterflies can be ephemeral. Because they are largely "solar powered," they can at times be hard to spot. But when found, these glittering, winged jewels can enliven any habitat or neighborhood. Butterflies seem to energize their environment in a way few other creatures can, save the brightest and most active of birds. We have greatly enjoyed butterflies for many years and invite you to join us in the delightful and satisfying pastime of butterfly watching. We hope, armed with knowledge of how to spot and understand butterflies, that you will enjoy and relish these enchanting creatures as much as we have.

— *Patricia and Clay Sutton*
Cape May, New Jersey

PART ONE

An Introduction to Butterfly Watching

Butterfly Basics

THE MIDMORNING SKIES over the Everglades held promise. Billowing cumulus began to form, hinting of lift, of good soaring conditions that should bring Anhingas, Wood Storks, and White Pelicans. It was a promise not to be realized. Only a few vultures and a single Red-shouldered Hawk circled high overhead.

Butterfly watching opens the doors to southern specialties such as Ruddy Daggerwing *(above),* **the tiny American Copper** *(right),* **and the large Eastern Tiger Swallowtail** *(previous page).*

Even yesterday's Short-tailed Hawk seemed but a distant memory. It was late March and Anhinga Trail was dead. An ongoing drought left the pools mostly dried up — only a few coots paddled desultorily about.

We were discouraged. Memories of the bounty of the Florida Everglades from trips in the mid-1970s seemed just that — distant memories never to be realized again. In 1991, Everglades restoration efforts had yet to come to fruition. Wading birds were few and far between. Remembered lush roadside ponds and ditches, teeming with spoonbills, egrets, and ibis, were dry and empty. The River of Grass and its attendant wildlife seemed as if from another lifetime. In short, the birding was poor, and far from home, we couldn't just go back and attend to chores.

Pat, remembering birds and bugs from years past, suggested Gumbo Limbo Trail. The lush vegetation to some degree masked the drought, and it was cool and shady on the trail. "I remember Zebras here in 1976," she reminisced. We were both beginning naturalists then and had needed to use a field guide to look up this striking long-

winged black butterfly with yellow stripes.

As we headed down the trail, and then took the path cutting over to the Old Ingraham Highway, we were soon enthralled by not one but a dozen Zebras, still dew-covered in their loose communal roost. We stood captivated, not breaking our gaze until a White Peacock floated by, pausing briefly to nectar. As the sun rose higher the trail became alive. Cloudless Sulphurs dashed by. "This one's different — wow, this must be a Large Orange Sulphur." "Look, a Queen!" Watching a Gulf Fritillary, with sparkling silver teardrops below, hover around a passion-vine we walked over to find a tiny yellow egg it had just laid. Further exploration revealed Gulf Fritillary caterpillars, orange with black stripes and bristles, on another passion-vine nearby.

Birds remained scarce, so we continued to concentrate on butterflies. It was a mind-opening adventure. Tiny Ceraunus Blues and huge Ruddy Daggerwings while we hiked on the Old Farm Road, cryptic Florida Leafwings and jewellike Georgia Satyrs while we bicycled the Long Pine Key Nature Trail, tiny but beautiful Phaon Crescents and Eastern Pygmy-Blues on the Coastal Prairie Trail near Flamingo.

The highlight came when following up a remembered tip from a friend. "When you're in the Everglades, try for Atalas near the bathroom at the Long Pine Key picnic area by the campground lake. You'll find abundant coontie there — their host plant — I saw a number of Atalas there last winter." It was unknown at the time if this was a natural colony or the result of successful reintroduction efforts for this spectacular tropical hairstreak.

Following these directions was almost too easy. We parked at the restroom, grabbed binoculars, and walked the road edge. We found the coontie easily. As quickly as we relate this, a butterfly whizzed by and perched.

Gulf Fritillaries *(above)* **range north to the Carolinas, but the Atala** *(below),* **a spectacular tropical hairstreak, is a true Florida specialty.**

How to Spot Butterflies

The steel blue wings, iridescent aquamarine spots, and red body glowed in the rich Florida light — an Atala. In the next hour or so we enjoyed, photographed, and were thrilled by about six different Atalas, a delectable tropical hairstreak making a welcome comeback in South Florida.

During the drive home, we reflected on the trip. The birding had been abysmal, the butterflying phenomenal. For us it was a watershed vacation. Butterfly watching had provided excitement, enjoyment, and challenges — a pattern that has repeated itself many times since. During tropical tours, we have been enthralled by butterflies in hotel gardens while marking time awaiting transportation to bird-rich sites. Along the Gulf Coast, after experiencing spectacular bird migration in the morning, we've turned to butterflies midday at their peak as bird action slowed. For us, butterflying doesn't replace birding, it beautifully complements it. Not either/or, but both.

Why Watch Butterflies?

People have studied butterflies for hundreds of years and for obvious reasons. Most are beautiful beyond belief. Some may be drab, but even then their camouflage makes finding them incredibly challenging. Some are so tiny, like the hairstreaks, that they seem to be part of the flowers they perch upon. Others are so specific to a particular brief season, habitat, or plant that finding them becomes a science or a quest. Take, for example, the Mitchell's Satyr, primarily found only in Michigan in certain sedge bogs. They are sin-

gle brooded, and adults fly for only about ten days in late June. What's more, they don't sing like birds, and can be found easily only on sunny days. Spotting one is a challenge and reward for any nature enthusiast.

Until fairly recently butterfly study has been done only with the use of a net and killing jar. In butterfly collecting, the perfect specimen was carefully pinned and mounted, usually along with dozens of others — possessed, but seldom watched. Butterfly watching, as opposed to collecting, first became popular in the 1980s, long after bird watching caught on, and is still in its infancy. It has been revolutionized by modern close-focus binoculars. Also, close-focus macro lenses for cameras now enable observers to document butterfly occurrences without collecting them; the auto-focus cameras of today are so sophisticated that just about anyone can take incredible photographs of butterflies.

Just as pioneer Ludlow Griscom, armed with crude binoculars, proved to gun-toting ornithologists that one did not have to shoot treetop warblers to identify them, recently some birders who are also butterfly enthusiasts have clearly demonstrated to net-carrying lepidopterists that butterflies don't have to be collected to be identified. Using all of the same observation skills so crucial to birding, coupled with today's binoculars and the many recently published excellent books on butterflies, butterfly watching has come of age.

Butterfly watching has many parallels to bird watching, and it is no surprise that birders everywhere are becoming bewitched by butterflies. The two activities need not exclude each other. In New Jersey, for example, where

Butterfly watching has been revolutionized by modern close-focus binoculars.

more than 430 species of birds have been seen, one need simply add 143 or so species of butterflies to the list of what to look for and enjoy.

Seasonality is a factor in butterfly watching just as it is in birding: knowing when to look for what. While by far best in the warmer months, butterfly watching is by no means just a summer pastime! On a warm winter day in late February you may be stunned to find a Mourning Cloak perched in a patch of sunlight on a pine forest floor. Some butterflies, such as Falcate Orangetip, can be found only in the very early spring. They commonly nectar on early blooming mustards in April. The elfins, named for their tiny size, are also found for only a brief time in the early spring. Many other butterflies, though, are not so limited in their seasonality and are common all summer and fall.

Continuing the analogy to birding, there can be dramatic migrations of some butterflies.

For example, on May 5, 1990, thousands of Red Admirals were seen surging north through the Cape May peninsula. Birders, scattered all over Cape May County enjoying a day's spring birding, couldn't help but notice them. In the fall the Monarch migration can be seen throughout much of North America.

Butterfly watching, like birding, can be as arduous or as relaxing as you wish. You can travel many miles to a specialized habitat, such as the tundra to enjoy far northern species of butterflies. Or you can go down the street to a weedy field or unmowed road shoulder in search of stands of swamp milkweed, Joe-pye-weed, common milkweed, and goldenrod and the assortment of butterflies they attract. Or, if you don't care to head out in search of butterflies, you can try to lure them to you by planting a garden brimming over with nectar sources all season long.

Butterfly watching has really taken off in

How to Spot Butterflies

the last few years. The resources available today make butterfly watching easier and more accessible than it was even just a few years ago. In Further Information (page 147) we've presented a mere sampling of the selection of resources available today, and the offering is growing day by day with new books being published in rapid succession. Field guides for butterfly watchers as opposed to butterfly collectors and regional guides with detailed accounts on habitat, larval foodplants, and life history are now readily available.

To begin butterfly watching for the first time, see if there is a butterfly checklist for your local area or region. It will give you a starting point by telling you what to look for and when and alerting you to how abundant, uncommon, or rare each species may be. Next, select one or several butterfly field guides, and perhaps annotate them with details gathered from a local checklist. Then clean your binoculars, and head out to your garden or a nearby weedy field.

If you like birding, you'll love butterflying. If you are not already a birder, you may become one after learning to use binoculars for butterflies. Be forewarned, though: butterfly watching can change your life and be one more wonderful excuse to go outdoors and explore.

Butterfly Biology

Learning to spot butterflies and enjoy them to the fullest hinges on an understanding of their basic biology and complex life history. Scientists classify all living plants and animals. Among animals, butterflies are in the invertebrate grouping. Among invertebrates, they

In North America moths, such as the Promethea Moth, outnumber butterfly species 14 to 1.

are placed in the arthropod phylum, which includes spiders, shrimps, crabs, insects, and others. Among the insect class there are many orders, such as beetles (Coleoptera), dragonflies and damselflies (Odonata), and moths and butterflies (Lepidoptera).

Lepidoptera means scaled wings, and moths and butterflies share this trait — they are soft-bodied insects with wings, body, and appendages covered with tiny scales. There are about 750,000 species (specific types) of insects worldwide, of which about 100,000–150,000 species are moths and about 15,000–20,000 species are butterflies. The vast majority of these are found in the tropics. In North America, 717 species of butterflies have been recorded north of Mexico, about 130 of which have occurred as strays or vagrants from the tropics. In North America, nearly 10,500 species of moths have been

Moths (Luna Moth, *left*) have feathery antennae that taper to a point; butterflies (Painted Lady, *right*) have thin antennae that swell at the tip, clublike.

recorded, outnumbering butterfly species fourteen to one.

The number of butterfly species in North America is very close to the number of bird species that are usually recorded in a given year, about 700. Flight periods of just a few days and the very limited ranges of some butterfly species make seeing 700 butterflies a far greater challenge than getting 700 birds on your life list.

In North America, the fewest species of butterflies occur in arctic regions, the most in subtropical areas such as southeastern Arizona and south Texas, where about 400 species have been recorded. No matter where you live there are probably about 100 species you can spot near home, more if you live in southern states, fewer if you live in the northern United States and Canada.

In the order Lepidoptera, butterflies differ considerably from moths, even though they may appear very similar to the eye. Moths have feathery or filamentous antennae that taper to a point, while butterflies have thin antennae that swell at the tip, clublike. Butterflies are diurnal, meaning active during the day, while most (but not all) moths are nocturnal, active only at night. Both use their antennae for smelling, but moths probably use them to a greater degree to find food and mates in the dark of night, whereas butterflies probably use vision to a greater degree. In general moths have hairier bodies than butterflies.

Another difference between moths and butterflies is the way their wings are joined. Moths have a tiny hook that fastens the forewing to the hindwing — hence their stiff, jerky flight compared to the more graceful flight of butterflies.

Scientists believe that moths first evolved from caddisflies and that butterflies evolved from moths. Of interest is that the primitive feature of hooking the wings together is still seen in one butterfly, the male of a skipper species found in Australia — providing the missing link. Butterflies as we know them probably came into existence about 150 million years ago in the Mesozoic era, about the same time as flowering plants. There has been a complex coevolution ever since. Charting their evolution has been difficult since soft body parts do not fossilize well. Through 1976 only about 41 butterfly fossils had ever been found worldwide.

Butterflies have a soft structure, but like all insects they have three body sections: the head, which contains mouthparts for feeding; the thorax, which anchors the wings and legs (all structures for locomotion); and the abdomen, which contains the digestive and reproductive organs.

The wing membranes are covered with millions of closely packed, socketed scales, like overlapping shingles on a roof. Scales protect the wing and are slowly lost over the life of an adult butterfly — some to predators, some to spider webs, and some to weather. Many slough off as wind whips branches and leaves around, knocking foliage into roosting or nectaring butterflies, or as rain strikes the butterfly. If you handle a butterfly, the powdery residue on your hands is scales. A tattered butterfly is often referred to by butterfliers as a "rag," as in ragged, and probably has but a few days yet to live.

Pigmented and faceted scales give the butterfly its color, a range of colors including all those seen by humans and some we cannot see, such as ultraviolet colors. Scales absorb certain wavelengths of light and reflect others. Some scales function like prisms, refracting the light and yielding rainbow colors — the iridescent and metallic colors of many of our more dramatic butterflies. Scales create the markings and patterns of butterflies, which are used as camouflage and to attract mates and repel predators. Were it not for

This newly emerged Red-spotted Purple with all its scales *(left)* is breathtaking. A tattered individual *(right)*, often referred to as a "rag," has but a few days to live.

Adult butterflies live very brief lives — long enough to mate, lay eggs on a suitable host plant, and die. This Spring Azure is laying her eggs on New Jersey tea.

their covering of scales, butterflies would be quite dull and probably held in no higher regard by man than most other insects. Instead, butterflies have long been revered in art, literature, and in our minds as symbols of all that is beautiful in the natural world.

To fully appreciate butterflies, it is important to understand key aspects of a butterfly's complex life cycle. Adult butterflies may fly for only a few days (in smaller species such as Spring Azure) or a few weeks. There are a few notable exceptions to this rule that we will highlight later. Most of a butterfly's life is spent becoming an adult.

All insects change in form as they grow, through a process called metamorphosis. But-

terflies (and moths) undergo complete metamorphosis in which there are four distinct stages: egg; larva (or caterpillar); pupa, also known as the chrysalis (called a cocoon in moths); and adult butterfly. Hormones circulating within the body trigger the changes that occur during the metamorphosis. In a process still not fully understood by scientists, the chrysalis turns to liquid and reconstitutes itself as an adult butterfly. This transformation is one wherein the tissues and structure of the caterpillar break down, then reform into the structure of the adult butterfly, one of the true miracles of nature.

After mating, adult butterflies lay eggs on suitable host plants. Some species lay eggs singly on plants, one egg per plant or one egg per leaf. Other species lay clusters of eggs. Eggs normally hatch within a few days. When the tiny caterpillar hatches from the egg, it is an eating machine, feeding on its host plant and growing larger and larger. The caterpillar stage of a butterfly's life is when the butterfly does all its growing. As the caterpillar grows too large for its skin, it sheds it and the new soft skin hardens, a process that will occur several times. These stages are known as instars, and the caterpillar can look very different in each instar. For example, a young (first instar) Black Swallowtail is black with a white saddle — a cryptic pattern that resembles a bird dropping, a camouflage to protect it from predators. Later instars look entirely different in color and pattern: they are green with black bands and yellow dots. After growing to full size, normally around two to three weeks, most caterpillars spin a silken thread that attaches them to safe sites. The caterpillar then becomes dormant, metamorphosing into the pupa. The outer surface of this pupa, or chrysalis, hardens, and the butterfly slowly develops inside. After two to three weeks (normally), the newly formed butterfly flexes its way out of the chrysalis and emerges as an adult butterfly. Initially the wings are greatly reduced in size. The butterfly pumps fluids into the wings until they expand or stretch out to their full size. After several hours the wings dry and the butterfly can fly. Every scale is fresh and perfect. It is fun to realize that when you see a perfectly intact, bright and beautiful butterfly, it has probably just recently emerged from its chrysalis. It will grow no larger, but its appearance may change as scales are worn or lost and it begins to fade.

Think of the caterpillar as the immature stage and the flying butterfly as the adult stage. Normally, the individual spends far more time as an egg, caterpillar, and chrysalis than it does as an adult — hence the statement that butterflies spend most of their time *becoming* a flying adult.

Adults also feed, not by chewing vegetation as did the caterpillar, but by drinking nectar from flowering plants. Some species of butterflies do not nectar, but obtain moisture and nutrients from wet soil, rotting fruit, animal feces and carcasses, or tree sap. An adult butterfly's primary purpose is to reproduce — to locate a suitable mate and go through the mating process. Mating may take up to 10 or 15 hours in some species. Butterflies can often be seen "in tandem," sitting or even flying while linked together. Most butterflies probably lay about 100 to 300 eggs, but some lay

A Zabulon Skipper's very long proboscis is suited for deep, tubular flowers.

Black Swallowtail Life Cycle —

1) DAY 1: egg on parsley;
2) DAY 6: caterpillar hatches;
3) DAY 18: caterpillar nearly full size;
4) DAY 20: caterpillar metamorphoses into a chrysalis;
5, 6) DAY 34 (2 photos): newly formed butterfly emerges and pumps liquids into wings.
7) Adult butterfly can now fly and begin this cycle anew.

---

as few as a dozen and others lay more than a thousand. After mating and laying eggs, the adult dies.

Most individuals of a generation, through all their life stages, live about one year. The lengths of each life stage, however, differ widely. In some species, individuals spend most of their lives as an egg, other species as a caterpillar, others yet as a chrysalis, and more rarely some species live longest as adults. Here we need to understand the complex issues of seasonality and broods. Some species are multibrooded — that is, they go through the entire life cycle (egg to caterpillar to chrysalis to adult) several times a year. These species are said to have several broods, or generations, each year; the adults of these are said to have a number of flight periods. This occurs in species found mostly in warm climates, yet some butterflies in temperate zones also have several broods each year. Other species will have only one brood per year. Henry's Elfin, for example, will have only one brood each year whether in Nova Scotia or in Florida. Some butterflies, Eastern Tiger Swallowtail for example, may have several broods in the South but are single-brooded at the northern limit of their range and at high altitudes, where cold weather impinges on growth and metamorphosis. Think of it as many variations on a theme.

Over much of the country the Black Swallowtail is an example of a double-brooded butterfly. Adults fly from mid-April to mid-June,

---

Once butterflies, such as these Eastern Tailed Blues, mate and lay eggs to create the next generation, they will die.

during which time they mate, lay eggs, and die. Their eggs hatch May through June, depending on when they were laid. Caterpillars feed, grow, and eventually pupate, some by mid-June and others as late as late July. The second brood of adults emerges from these pupae between late June and late August. They mate, lay eggs, and die. By mid-September not one adult Black Swallowtail can be found. Their eggs hatch, and the caterpillars feed and grow. By mid-August some caterpillars have grown to full size and pupated. Caterpillars that hatched from eggs laid in late August will not pupate until early October. Pupae or chrysalids from this second brood all overwinter. The following April, the next year's first brood of adults emerges from these chrysalids. Understand that this is average

timing. It may differ a bit in your area. Sometimes, too, a few individuals are out of sync. For some species the last very worn individuals of the first brood may in fact overlap with fresh, newly emerged second-brood adults.

Consider, on the other hand, the single-brooded Henry's Elfin, an early spring butterfly. The adult emerges from the pupa in early spring. Some individuals may live for only a week or so, particularly if they encounter cold or wet weather (males generally live the shortest times). The adult must quickly mate and lay eggs. The eggs hatch and larvae feed for about a month on flowers and young leaves, then pupate on the host plant or in sand or leaf litter at the base of the host plant. The pupa goes into diapause, a state of complete physiological arrest in which no de-

Mourning Cloaks are thought to be the longest-lived adult butterflies in North America.

How to Spot Butterflies

velopment occurs. It remains in this resting stage for ten months or longer, until the adult emerges the following spring. A Henry's Elfin may emerge and fly in late February in the Florida prairies, but those in Nova Scotia will emerge in mid-June.

In New Jersey, individual Henry's Elfins may be seen from early April to mid-May. Even though an individual adult may live only a week or so, emergence of various adults is staggered over time — a strategy designed to ensure survival, so that not all adults can be wiped out by a single bad weather event. The Common Wood-Nymph has a particularly protracted flight period. It has one flight (single-brooded), yet can be seen from mid-June to mid-September most years. This is because the emergence of individuals is scattered over time and some individuals estivate during part of the summer.

Over most of its range the Mourning Cloak is another example of a single-brooded butterfly (in the South it has been reported to have two broods). Eggs laid in late April hatch in May. Caterpillars feed, grow, and eventually pupate (go into the chrysalis form) in June. Adults emerge in late June or July. During hot weather they may spend several weeks or even months in estivation, a state of inactivity, while waiting for cooler weather. They become active again in fall, and many migrate south. Adults overwinter by hibernating — a deep sleep in a protected spot where their metabolism slows down through the cold winter months. Warm winter days may seduce a hibernating Mourning Cloak to wake up and fly about, but only briefly if the temperature drops again. With spring's warmth they come out of hibernation fully and become active again, and some migrate north. They mate in April and May and then die. The process continues anew. Mourning Cloaks are thought to be the longest-lived adult butterflies in North America, and some adults may live for as long as ten or eleven months.

Many beginning butterfly enthusiasts make the mistake of looking for a simple answer, seeking a simple understanding of the life cycle of all butterflies. In reality, it can be quite complex. The development of a butterfly from egg to adult can take anywhere from three weeks to several years. The shortest life cycles are in warm tropical areas. Some Arctic species, such as the Jutta Arctic, are biennial species. Young larvae (first to third instar) hibernate the first winter. Older larvae (fourth to sixth instar) hibernate the second winter. Individual adults therefore fly only in the second year of the life of the generation, although some adults are on the wing every year.

Time spent with the books will be time well spent if you hope to sort out butterfly life cycles. Head to the books after each new sighting, taking it species by species. There are many strategies, many variations, every one fascinating, all miraculous.

Butterflies and Botany

How often have you been with a naturalist and marveled at his or her knowledge of just about *everything*? Factual descriptions roll off the tongue, such as, "the Red-spotted Purple is perched in the wild cherry tree, left of the gall on the main branch." You, the observer, are able to actually find the butterfly and are

A nectaring Baltimore Checkerspot is never far from turtlehead, its host plant.

grateful that it was not pointed out as being "over there" or "in the tree over there" when an entire forest lies before you. As you look up Red-spotted Purple in your field guide you might be even more impressed to learn that wild cherry is the host plant most frequently used by this butterfly. The direct link between butterflies and plants continues as the naturalist points out that "a Tawny Emperor just flew out of the hackberry tree" or shares that "this patch of willows often produces Viceroys." Once you have learned how closely butterflies are tied to specific plants, not just their favored nectar sources, but also essential larval foodplants, your ability to find, identify, and even garden successfully for butterflies will take off!

You can't know butterflies without first learning a bit about botany. Adult butterflies lay eggs on suitable host plants, also known as larval foodplants. Butterfly larvae feed on the plant's buds, leaves or needles, and developing fruits and flowers. The important thing to remember is that butterflies are host specific. When we speak of a larval foodplant or a host plant, we mean that species of plant which a particular butterfly species requires or selects.

Some butterflies can use a number of larval foodplants. The Gray Hairstreak uses a wide variety of plants and as a result is one of the commonest and most widely distributed butterflies in North America. Cabbage Whites may use a variety of species, but all are in the Mustard family. Other butterflies are extremely host specific. Hoary Elfin caterpillars eat only bearberry; Bog Copper caterpillars can survive only on cranberry; Hessel's Hairstreak caterpillars eat only white cedar. Harris' Checkerspot caterpillars feed only on flat-topped white aster even though many other asters are available where they occur.

Adult female butterflies often select the proper larval foodplant by smelling and tasting

How to Spot Butterflies

various plants. They smell with their antennae, and they "taste" for the proper foodplant with sensory receptors on their feet, a remarkable adaptation. They lay the eggs on only that host plant, so that hatching caterpillars can begin to feed right away. For host-specific species, the caterpillar will not eat and will not survive unless it has the proper foodplant to feed on.

Butterfly field guides generally list known larval foodplants. For rarer species, a knowledge of the host plant and how to identify it is essential for finding the butterfly. We had never seen a Baltimore Checkerspot in New Jersey until early one June, when we came upon turtlehead, its only host plant, while hiking through a highlands bog. We made a point of returning to the turtlehead stand in late June, the only known flight period for this single-brooded species, and bingo! We enjoyed a dozen spectacular, freshly emerged Baltimores.

It is quite fun to learn plants and habitat types through the butterflies. When finding a new butterfly, search until you find the host plant, often nearby. Learning habitats is important too. Certain bogs hold Appalachian Browns, other types of bogs have the "wrong" plant associations. In southern coastal salt marshes do not expect Eastern Pygmy-Blues unless you see glasswort, their only host plant.

Adult butterflies drink the sugary nectar from flowers with a long, coiled, extendable and retractable tonguelike proboscis. Nectar sources are never so specific as host plants. Monarchs lay eggs only on milkweed, but will nectar on a wide variety of plants. The length of a butterfly's proboscis does determine which flowers it can nectar on. Deep, tubular flowers attract butterflies with an extremely long proboscis, such as skippers and swallowtails. Typically butterflies that are attracted to sap have a short proboscis. Butterflies see all the colors we see plus the ultraviolet range of colors. Some species seem to be more partial to certain-colored flowers than others. Begin to take note of which nectar sources are irresistible to butterflies in general and to particular species of butterflies. It can be very helpful during field trips and in planning a butterfly garden.

Keep a diary of your observations. Your eye will grow keener as you look over a landscape. Rather than simply looking for fields, you'll be looking for fields and roadsides hosting certain wildflowers irresistible to butterflies: milkweeds, goldenrods, knapweed, asters, thistles, coreopsis, wild bergamot, ironweed, coneflowers, clovers, and more.

Eastern Pygmy-Blues lay eggs on glasswort, their only host plant.

Your greatest compliment and satisfaction will come when asked how you identified a particular butterfly and you realize that it was by association with the plants it was flitting around! A love of butterflies will, of necessity, lead to an interest in botany. Your wildflower guide and tree and shrub guide will soon occupy your car's back seat, next to your well-worn butterfly field guides.

Butterfly Ecology

Butterflies play a significant role in the ecology of their habitat. Butterflies and moths rank second only to bees as beneficial pollinators of fruits and other crops. They pollinate flowering plants by carrying pollen from plant to plant on mouthparts, legs and feet, and even on their wings. We have seen Eastern Tiger Swallowtails stained completely orange with the pollen of Turk's-cap lilies. Certain butterfly caterpillars, when concentrated and in the absence of predators, can sometimes defoliate host plants, but this is very unusual.

Butterfly populations fluctuate greatly from year to year, often for reasons not understood. Drought can have significant effects on butterflies, mainly by impacting their host and nectar plants. Obviously, larval foodplants and nectar sources will flourish or struggle as a result of rainfall or the lack thereof. Poor nectar availability can affect the survival of adult butterflies and their reproductive success.

Heavy rainfall, high winds, cold weather, and snowfall can affect butterflies. For many years we've noted fewer flying butterflies after any major storm, and it can take days or a week or so before numbers recover through the emergence of new individuals. Early spring storms, low temperatures, and snowfall can cause high mortality of early emerging species. One year, a very late frost in our region killed all the budding oak leaves. Many oak-specific butterfly species were affected. The oaks rebudded, but timing was off to meet butterfly needs.

Sometimes population fluctuations seem unrelated to any known cause. Several years ago, we saw hundreds of 'Olive' Juniper Hairstreaks locally, large numbers of each of the three broods. The following year, we saw none at all, with only two or three reported by local butterfliers. The third year was an average year and we again saw dozens, but certainly not hundreds. Many population fluctuations remain unexplained, but the butterfly watcher will come to realize that every year is different, with large numbers of one butterfly species and few of another. Such variations are one of the fascinations of butterfly spotting.

A great many predators feed on butterflies at every stage of their life cycle. Birds are one of the primary predators of caterpillars, gleaning tiny and large caterpillars from leaves, but many insects take a toll too. Parasitic wasps and flies commonly lay eggs on the eggs and caterpillars of both moths and butterflies; when the wasp or fly larvae hatch, they penetrate and consume the egg or caterpillar from within, eventually killing it. Many different insects prey on adult butterflies. If you garden you're sure to find butterflies in the clutches of praying mantises, robber flies, assassin bugs, ambush bugs, dragonflies, and wasps to name a few. Many times we have found a praying mantis in our garden by first

before our eyes. Spiders prey on butterflies too. Some catch butterflies large and small in their webs. Crab spiders wait in ambush atop flower heads for an unsuspecting butterfly to land and nectar. Birds, lizards, frogs, toads, and even mice are opportunistic predators and will feed on butterflies. It's a jungle out there!

Butterflies have evolved many strategies to avoid predators. Cryptic coloration is used by many — even by some that are brightly patterned. A Red Admiral is a blaze of colors when its wings are spread, but when it closes them, it is remarkably camouflaged and can blend into the pattern of a tree trunk.

Predators feed on every stage of a butterfly's life. Parasitic wasps and flies lay eggs on caterpillars. The praying mantis is a major predator of adult butterflies.

noticing a pile of Monarch wings on the ground below a flower head where the mantis was lying in wait for the next victim. An Eastern Pondhawk dragonfly once plucked a Common Wood-Nymph out of the air right

Many butterflies are cryptically colored to avoid predators. A Red Admiral is a blaze of color on top, but when it closes its wings it blends in beautifully with a tree trunk.

Leafwings, anglewings, tortoiseshells, and the American Snout all look inanimate when they land, like a dead leaf or twig or a bit of bark. Mimicry, wherein one butterfly's pattern mimics another, is widely used by butterflies in the tropics. In the temperate region, the Viceroy's similarity to the unpalatable Monarch (distasteful to most birds because of its milkweed diet in the caterpillar stage) is the best-known example of mimicry.

Many butterflies have eyespots on their wings. These spots are thought to cause some predators, birds or bugs, to pause, thinking they are about to attack a much larger, more formidable opponent. A second theory, perhaps better, is that predators aim for the eyespots when trying to grab a butterfly, but get only a piece of wing, not the head of the prey like they expected. Some butterflies have "tails," which are actually protrusions from the wings, thought to look like or imitate antennae. The tails on swallowtails are often missing thanks to predators. Many hairstreaks rub their hindwings back and forth so that predators aim for the "false head" (eyespots and tails) and get only a piece of wing. A butterfly missing only a chunk of wing escapes relatively unscathed. As long as the butterfly body remains intact it can still mate, lay eggs, and create the next generation — the primary purpose of the adult stage.

Many caterpillars are patterned or camouflaged to deter predators. Early instars of some swallowtails look precisely like inedible bird droppings. Older instars of some swallowtails have large eyespots that may startle and frighten off predators. Some caterpillars are colored and patterned so like their host plant that they blend in and are all but impossible to see. This is especially true of the coppers, hairstreaks, and blues. A number of caterpillars, such as the Gulf Fritillary and

The Viceroy *(right)* **is so similar in color and pattern to the distasteful Monarch** *(left)* **that most predators avoid it. This defense is known as mimicry. This Black Swallowtail caterpillar** *(below)* **has extended its osmeterium to deter predators.**

Question Mark caterpillars, have bristly, thorny projections to deter interested birds or lizards. Swallowtail caterpillars take it a step further by assuming threatening postures and extending a bright orange forked scent gland, known as the "osmeterium," which emits a pungent odor. Even we are deterred from picking them up!

Butterfly Behavior

An understanding of basic butterfly behavior is essential for the butterfly watcher. Knowing what they are probably going to be doing at various times of the day can greatly increase your chances of finding them. Butterflies are cold-blooded, which means their body temperature is dependent upon the surrounding air temperature. Most cannot fly until temperatures warm to 55° or 60°F. On a cool morning, in order to fly, butterflies need to warm up the thoracic muscles that control their wings. To warm their thorax (body), they

Some caterpillars startle or frighten off predators with eyespots *(above)*. **Eastern Tiger Swallowtail** *(right)* **nectaring on common milkweed. Swallowtails are among the first butterflies to become active in the morning.**

commonly bask. Basking, or "sunbathing," can quickly raise the body temperature, just like it does for snakes and lizards, and even poolside people. There are various types of basking. Lateral baskers tilt sideways, with closed wings, turning the ventral (underside) surface of the hindwings perpendicular to the sun's warmth. Sulphurs are lateral baskers. Swallowtails, anglewings, and Monarchs are dorsal baskers, sunbathing with their wings fully open and the dorsal or top surface exposed to and angled toward the sun. Blues and hairstreaks are body baskers, angling their wings so that the sun hits the body to the greatest degree, and many use conduction basking — warming up by pressing the body to a warm surface, such as gravel or roads, in order to conduct heat directly.

Once the thorax has warmed up, to about 82°F, the butterfly is ready to fly. In the sun and out of the wind, this can sometimes be achieved even if the ambient air temperature is only 50–55°F. During the course of the day, it seems almost as if a butterfly is regulated by a thermostat. If a Painted Lady is dorsal basking in sunlight, and a cloud covers the sun, it will quickly close its wings to retard heat loss. As soon as the sun reappears, it will instantly reopen its wings. Butterflies need to avoid overheating as well, and sometimes they will close their wings even in sunlight — to prevent too much heat build-up. On summer days, when midday temperatures are the highest, butterflies may retire to shady areas and become inactive, a type of roosting. They retreat out of the sun to the undersides of leaves within vegetated borders or dense shady forest. In our garden there is always a pronounced midday lull in activity during hot summer days. In colder weather, seek butterflies in sunny edges out of the wind. On the hottest days, go butterflying early in the morning; midday look for butterflies in cooler, shady areas.

It is interesting that the amount of sunshine that a region receives in part determines how many butterfly species occur there. The British Isles have 58 species of butterflies, of which only 32 occur regularly in Ireland. In the United States, New Jersey has more sunny weather and 143 species have been recorded. Texas, Arizona, and New Mexico, with their near tropical climate, have recorded the highest numbers in North America. Texas has recorded about 423 species, Arizona about 328 species, and New Mexico about 321 species. The Pacific Northwest, with its well-known cool, rainy climate, lacks the butterfly diversity of inland areas at the same latitude.

Adult Mourning Cloaks, anglewings, and tortoiseshells estivate during the hotter months of midsummer, becoming completely inactive for weeks at a time. They also hibernate as adults through the winter, sheltered in hollow logs or trees, stone walls, outbuildings, and wood piles.

Puddling is another interesting butterfly behavior. Many species, and particularly the males, congregate in damp sandy spots, puddle edges, seeps, and pond edges. These congregations are often referred to as "mud-puddle parties." Here they drink, but also ingest nutrients and salts along with the water. Some species seem to be gregarious, with dozens of the same species puddling together. Other times a mix of species can be found.

Hilltopping is another fascinating butterfly behavior. After morning feeding, males of many species fly to the highest area around, at times traveling great distances to a hilltop, cliff, or ridge. Here they seek a good view to watch for females and rival males. From a command-

This Two-tailed Swallowtail is puddling to get salts from the damp ground.

ing view, they fly out to investigate passing butterflies. Unmated females seek males at these locations. Hairstreaks are notorious hilltoppers. Hilltopping occurs in many forms — you may often find a butterfly at the highest point in your own garden. Place a long twig among lower flowers, and butterflies will invariably perch there (and afford good photo opportunities). In relatively flat areas treetopping replaces hilltopping. In an urban seaside town with very few trees and no hills, we've watched hairstreaks hilltop from a flagpole.

Patrolling is another butterfly behavior that you will often notice while afield. Male butterflies of many species commonly stake out territories along edges or along woods roads. They fly back and forth, returning to one or more favored perches. They patrol looking for females. Rival males are chased away in frenetic dogfights. Duskywings are constant patrollers. Along sandy roads through oak woods you may very well encounter one patrolling Juvenal's Duskywing after another. When males encounter each other where two territories meet, swirling chases occur.

In our garden, Silver-spotted Skippers are quite territorial, chasing not only other males but also Monarchs and swallowtails. We've even seen them give chase to hummingbirds and Great-crested Flycatchers — seemingly risky business.

The alert spotter can frequently observe courtship behavior. Male butterflies almost always make the first move. Perchers wait for females to enter their territory, while patrollers actively search for females. The initial encounter occurs in the air. Females may be unreceptive if they have already mated and are instead focused on laying eggs. Uninterested females display their rejection in a number of ways: by flying away, by flying straight up into the air, by perching and quivering their wings, or by perching with the abdomen held vertically in the air so that the male cannot mate with them. Receptive females alight and the mating ritual begins. Pheromones, produced by both sexes, stimulate the act of mating. Some males flutter their wings to send their pheromones toward the receptive female. Most females mate once and spend the rest of their brief lives searching for suitable host plants and laying their eggs on these plants. Male butterflies may mate with four or five females in their brief lives, and some species with more than a dozen females. Mating may be brief — a few minutes — or quite prolonged — a few hours — with paired butterflies flying in tandem, abdomen to abdomen.

Migration

Many butterfly species are sedentary. Bog Coppers and Baltimore Checkerspots don't move more than a few hundred feet from where they were born (although some individuals must disperse some years or isolated bogs would never be populated by the butterflies). Other butterflies are migratory, and this migration can take many forms.

Migration is any seasonal movement between two areas. It is found throughout the animal kingdom and is prevalent among insects. Migration can be for the purpose of obtaining food, or escaping the colder temperatures of winter. For butterflies it can be a combination of both. Many species of butterflies are migratory, some to a much greater degree than others. The Monarch is the best-known, most complex, and longest-distance migrant. Its migration is the greatest migration of any butterfly worldwide, and one of the true wonders of the natural world.

Other butterflies also make impressive migrations. The Painted Lady moves great distances. Adults cannot survive northern winters north of the southwestern United States and Mexican deserts. In spring and early summer they surge northward, repopulating the United States. Some years there may be four or five broods in their summer range, other years one or two. Then the offspring of those that arrived in the spring and early summer will migrate south in the fall. After harsh winters they may be absent from the eastern United States, as they were for several years after the severely cold and snowy winter of 1995–96 that affected areas as far

Common Buckeye *(left)* **is a regular migrant, while the Long-tailed Skipper** *(right)* **is an emigrant and performs a one-way migration north.**

south as Florida. Common Buckeyes, not known to winter north of coastal North Carolina, move north each spring. Each fall at Cape May they are the second-commonest butterfly after Monarchs, implying a return to the South, although this is not well studied.

Some species whose adults can survive northern winters in hibernation (Question Mark, Red Admiral, and Mourning Cloak) show migratory tendencies as well. Noticeable numbers migrate south in the fall and north again in the spring, supplementing the populations of those that stayed behind.

Migration is an exciting event for the butterfly watcher. At Cape May in September and October, when prevailing autumn westerly winds combine to create amazing butterfly concentrations along the beachfronts (since butterflies avoid, when possible, flying over water), sometimes thousands of Monarchs,

hundreds of Common Buckeyes, and dozens of Painted Ladies, American Ladies, and Question Marks can be seen moving south. A few sulphurs, Eastern Commas, and Mourning Cloaks are usually mixed in — an amazing spectacle as they move south with the sun.

In late summer, some southern butterflies perform an irregular one-way migration north. In the Northeast we eagerly await Cloudless Sulphurs, Little Yellows, Sleepy Oranges, Variegated Fritillaries, Long-tailed Skippers, Clouded Skippers, Fiery Skippers, Sachems, and Ocola Skippers every August and September. These emigrations (leaving one area to migrate) usually follow good breeding seasons to the south, and it has been theorized that the adult butterflies may be reacting to an overpopulation and stressed food resources (nectar and/or larval foodplants).

How to Spot Butterflies

Southern species fly north to eventually die, however. There is no corresponding southbound migration known for these species. They may rear a brood far to the north of their normal range, but they and their offspring are eventually doomed by falling temperatures. These movements are unpredictable, some years involving none, dozens, or hundreds of individuals.

In the West, American Snouts are known for their dramatic mass emigrations, also called irruptions. Some years very few are seen north of their permanent range; other years, millions upon millions move north, and there are reports of them darkening the sky and of motorists having to pull over because so many snouts were smashed on the windshield that they couldn't see.

It's these irruptive species that make for exciting watching opportunities. Strays or vagrants far from their normal range add an element of surprise, and all butterfly watchers anxiously anticipate and learn to look for them each season. A Compton Tortoiseshell, of northern forests, creates a stir when found in southern New Jersey. A Long-tailed Skipper, whose caterpillars are sometimes serious pests of bean crops in the Deep South, is a major event when found at Jamaica Bay NWR near New York City.

Migration is an exciting aspect of butterfly spotting. We can never forget an autumn day on the beach near Georgetown, South Carolina, when we watched hundreds of Monarchs resolutely moving southwest, striving for Mexican mountains. Against this, and passing in midair, were hundreds of Cloudless Sulphurs and Gulf Fritillaries, every single one heading due north. The sulphurs and fritillaries were emigrating, heading north to a fate unknown. The Monarchs were toiling south, navigating somehow to a place they had never been, a place their great-great-great-grandparents had come from more than six months before.

During migration Monarchs gather at evening roosts out of the wind. Sometimes hundreds or more roost together.

Equipment

T WASN'T LONG AGO that butterfly study demanded a lot of paraphernalia: butterfly net, glassine envelopes, jars, chemicals, and substantial storage space for the collection. In this age of environmental consciousness and awareness of environmental threats, it is far more ethical and nonconsumptive to watch and enjoy but-

Modern close-focus binoculars *(right)* are necessary to see the gorgeous details, patterns, and colors on butterflies, especially the small hairstreaks such as this Great Purple Hairstreak *(above).*

terflies rather than collect them and add to their plight. There are valid reasons for scientists to collect butterflies, whether for taxonomic and scientific study or for exploration of tropical regions. But there is little reason for casual hobby collecting.

What has enabled the evolution of butterfly watching (and thus eliminated the net, making it as antiquated as shotguns are for bird watching) is the advent of modern close-focusing binoculars. While you may sometimes get within inches of a basking or feeding butterfly, this is the exception rather than the rule. Most identifications will be possible only after close-up views through your binoculars. If you are serious about wanting to enjoy butterflies, invest in a good-quality pair of binoculars.

For butterfly watching the lower-power binoculars are best: 7× (7-power), 8×, and some 10× models. Magnification, usually called "power," determines how close an object will appear and what details will be seen. In 8×42 binoculars, the first number stands for the power of magnification: 8× binoculars will bring an object eight

times closer to the viewer and make it appear that many times larger. A butterfly 16 feet away will thus appear to be only 2 feet away.

Brightness is also a critical variable in selecting binoculars. The amount of light a binocular draws in depends largely on the size of the front (objective) lenses and is denoted by the number following the multiplication sign. In 8×42 binoculars, the 42 indicates the size of the objective lens in millimeters. The larger the objective lens, the greater its light-gathering capability. Ongoing advancements in methods and types of optical coatings have resulted in brighter and brighter images. The more expensive binoculars utilize the best coatings to allow the most light transfer. Beware: these precious coatings that make some binoculars so expensive can be rubbed off or scratched if cleaned with your shirttail or a tissue. But with proper care and careful cleaning, binoculars are a lifetime investment.

Also consider a binocular's field of view, the amount of area that will be visible edge to edge. Because butterfly spotting involves a good deal of scanning ahead and following quick-moving individuals, wide-angle binoculars are best.

Eyeglass wearers need to be sure the binoculars they select offer sufficient eye relief (15–20 mm of depth between the lens and the top of the eye cup). This is closely related to field of view. Fold or pop down the rubber eye cups to get your eyeglass lenses close to the binocular's ocular lenses to enjoy a wide field of view.

The absolutely critical factor in choosing binoculars for butterfly watching is that they be close-focus. To paraphrase an old joke, there are three critical factors: 1) close-focus, 2) close-focus, and 3) close-focus. This is why your great-grandfather's war surplus hand-me-downs are not going to work for spotting butterflies. Most birding binoculars, even modern quality brands, focus to only 12 or 15 feet. This is not good enough for butterfly watching, since many butterflies are tiny and often spotted as they flush and land again, quite close but not close enough to see well with your naked eye. You do not want to have to back up to get a butterfly in focus, since by doing so the butterfly image gets smaller, defeating your purpose of using binoculars to enlarge the image in the first place.

For butterfly watching, a binocular needs to focus on objects 7 to 8 feet away; 5 or 6 feet is even better. Many butterfly watchers prefer mini or pocket close-focus binoculars, partly for the light weight and partly because they also carry camera gear and it is easy and convenient to, just as the name implies, stash the binoculars in a pocket while taking pictures.

A number of optic companies are perfecting binoculars with butterfly watchers in mind. Test different models and makes for yourself to see which you prefer. Consider size, weight, brightness, clarity, how close they focus, field of view, whether they give effective eye relief for eyeglass wearers, and of course, price. Popular butterfly binoculars in use today include Bausch & Lomb 8×42 Elite (focus to 4.8 feet), Bausch & Lomb 7×26 Custom Compact (focus to 7 feet), Bausch & Lomb 10×42 Elite (focus to 5.2 feet), Cabela's 10×42 (focus to 4.8 feet), Celestron 8×42 Regal (focus to 4.7 feet), Minolta 8×22 Pocket (focus to 5.8 feet), Minolta 10×25 Pocket (focus to 5.8 feet), Swift 8×25 (focus to 6.6 feet), and Pentax 7×20 (focus to 6.2 feet). All are good and will do the job; discounted prices vary from around $800 down to about $100. Naturally, the higher-priced models will be brighter, more water-resistant, and longer lasting. We recommend you visit your local nature center, one that sells quality optics, and try various models to see which fits your needs and budget.

We used Zeiss 7×42 binoculars for years, for both birding and butterflying. They are top birding binoculars and certainly adequate for butterflies, focusing to 8 feet. Recently, however, we both switched to Bausch & Lomb Elite 8×42 binoculars, which focus to 4.8 feet — you can focus on your toes. As professional naturalists, we use our binoculars for just about everything: birds, butterflies, dragonflies, whales, wolves, and even fish watching! Our butterfly binoculars must double as birding binoculars. The Bausch & Lomb Elite 8×42 are one of the few close-focus butterfly binoculars that are also stellar birding binoculars. It took some time getting used to the narrow depth of field when quickly focusing between distant birds and close butterflies, but with them we've enjoyed excellent looks at Parasitic Jaegers chasing Smith's Longspurs overhead while we watched Banded Alpines and Jutta Arctics on the tundra in Alaska's Arctic National Wildlife Refuge. In the mountains of Mexico they served us well as we focused on Red Warblers and Slate-throated Redstarts overhead and Monarchs at our feet. Even the most ardent butterfly enthusiasts occasionally watch birds, and with today's choices, you can find quality binoculars that you can easily use for both.

While we would never recommend that you buy a spotting scope for butterfly watching, if you already own a birding scope, don't leave it at home when you go butterflying. In Mexico, we set up our 30× scope to study a Bat Falcon that was perched across a deep, narrow ravine and discovered a blooming tree alive with butterflies near the falcon. With the tree canopy at eye level, we got a far better view than we ever could have from below. We used the scope to leisurely study the kaleidoscope of whirling and nectaring butterflies. Most were Hammock Skippers and White-tipped Pixies, along with a few Red-bordered Pixies and several Sailors. The prize was a beautiful and showy tailed metalmark that was a shimmery electric blue with red spots — the tropical *Rhetus arcius*. A bit closer to home a scope enabled us to study a patch of dogbane in a fenced-off pasture from 75 yards away and discover three nectaring Bronze Coppers, confirming only the second known colony at that time in southern New Jersey. Don't run out and buy a telescope just for butterfly watching, but if you have one, keep it handy. It will prove very useful if you lead butterfly walks too, allowing newcomers incredible looks that may hook them.

Photographing Butterflies

Little else is needed in the way of equipment for butterfly watching, but you may eventually want a camera to record and remember your finds. Photographs and slides can capture the razzle-dazzle beauty of butterflies that is so difficult to put into words. Your photos may put the "wow" into butterfly watching for a friend who has never taken a close look at them. Photographs can also be an excellent way to improve your identification skills. Every one of us has seen butterflies we can't identify. A good photo can be shown to friends and colleagues, passed around and discussed. Usually, an identification is arrived upon, and you've all learned a lot in the process. A photograph or slide can also serve as a scientific tool, technically recording butterfly occurrences for scientists, land managers, and conservationists.

Modern close-up photography equipment and techniques make it easy to photograph and document a rare butterfly, eliminating the need for a specimen record. Photographic

Gardeners' kneepads are invaluable as the butterfly photographer inches forward, low and slow so as not to flush the butterfly with one's shadow.

proof in response to skepticism has proved useful more than once.

For years we took out-of-focus, underexposed photos, most often with the subject so small it was hard to see. Finally we were convinced to invest in a camera set-up designed specifically for butterfly photography. *Anyone* can take excellent photos of butterflies with the equipment available today. We are living proof. We would much rather focus on butter-

fly watching and study than on photography. Our camera is a tool, an aside, not the reason we head out into the field. With the proper equipment it is easy to get excellent results with butterfly photography.

You will need a 35mm camera, a close-up, or macro, lens, and a flash. Only with a close-up lens will the butterfly fill the frame and be large enough to recognize and enjoy in the photo. Do not make the mistake of buying a zoom lens for bird photography expecting its macro feature to be satisfactory for butterflies up close. Zoom lenses and macro lenses are made differently and get very different results. The macro setting on a zoom lens will never capture a life size image; the largest you can hope for is one-third life size, and that is very limiting when so many butterflies are tiny. Because of the way the glass in a zoom lens is ground, edges of photos taken with the macro setting will be slightly out of focus. You will get far better butterfly photos with a macro lens. Macro lens glass is ground much more finely. The result is a sharp image edge to edge. A 100- or 105 mm macro lens will give you the best results by allowing you to focus close and capture life-size images of the butterfly. A macro lens is heavy and much more expensive than a zoom lens with macro capabilities, but the results are far superior. A flash is important, too. Fill flash is often needed, even on sunny days, both to stop movement and to bring out the intricate patterning of many butterfly species. Kneepads are worth their weight in gold to the butterfly photographer. To avoid flushing a butterfly and to get close enough for a photograph often necessitates getting down on a butterfly's level and slowly inching forward — often on one's knees. Some garden catalogs sell garden pants that have knee pockets to accommodate cushioning neoprene pads — which makes this maneuver painless.

While much butterfly spotting can be done from dry roads and trails, specialty species often require "getting wet" — hiking to and through wet meadows and bogs. For example, we have always had to slog through standing water to see Bog Coppers and Black Dashes. So, you may want to invest in a pair of knee-high rubber boots, though many prefer old sneakers to boots. Since butterflies are solar powered, remember your sunscreen as well. Oh yes, one final item: insect repellent. Not all insects are as benign and enjoyable as butterflies.

Finding Butterflies

WHY WATCH BUTTERFLIES? We doubt that it can be said any better than by Robert Michael Pyle in his landmark book, *Handbook for Butterfly Watchers*.

Seeking out and observing butterflies gives one a unique window on the world. One cannot become a butterfly lover without at the same time growing sensitive to the animals, plants, soils, landforms, weather, and climate — and the habitats they all make up together. So the watcher of butterflies soon becomes a botanist, a geologist, a reader of clouds — in effect, a general naturalist. I know of few pursuits out-of-doors that lead one quite as a matter of course down so many avenues. And this means that the lepidopterist gains as well an appreciation for the landscape as a whole and an understanding of the imperative for thoughtful and caring stewardship.

Understanding butterflies requires a matrix of skills, each dependent on the other. The study of butterflies leads to an understanding of plants — both larval foodplants and nectar plants — and habitats. These, in turn, will lead to a better understanding of

Butterfly study leads to an understanding of larval foodplants (Frosted Elfin, *above*, on its host plant, wild indigo) and nectar (Mormon Metalmark, *right*, on acacia).

44

how and where butterflies are found, or more simply, why they are found.

Finding butterflies beyond the bright, obvious, everyday species in flower gardens is rooted in an understanding of butterfly biology and natural history. We are fortunate to have a wide range of butterfly books available, and Further Information, p. 147, recommends some of our favorites, with annotations on their specific strengths. At the outset, time spent in an easy chair, perhaps on winter nights, learning all you can about lepidoptera, their habits and habitats, will be the most valuable tool.

To apply butterfly basics to butterfly finding, first focus on the simple fact that butterflies are solar powered. Temperatures need to be about 55°–60°F or higher for butterflies to be active. Butterflies are for people who like

nice weather. We like Ann Swengel's T-Shirt Rule: if it's comfortable to be outside in a T-shirt, it's a good butterfly day. The only time we have not found this to be true is in alpine or arctic habitats, where butterflies are adapted to colder weather.

If you can choose your days to be afield for butterflies, warm and sunny is the optimal condition. But such a day, with butterflies in abundance, can change abruptly with the arrival of cloud cover or overcast conditions. As if a switch has been thrown, diversity drops and many butterflies seem to evaporate with cloud cover. They are still there, but much more difficult to find because they have crawled down into vegetation to wait out the cloudy interlude. If the sun sneaks in and out of the clouds, you will find the sunny periods, no matter how brief, to be active with butterflies nectaring and flying, and, in comparison, the dark, cloudy stretches will be largely devoid of butterflies.

One of the charms of butterfly watching is that you don't need to be out at dawn to hit the peak period, as you do in birding. Areas to find butterflies usually need to be in full sunlight, generally with the sun at a high angle. Even in midsummer, many butterflies are rarely very active before 9:00 A.M. or after 5:00 P.M. Think of them as keeping bankers' hours. And, like bankers, they generally take a lunch break. In hot summer weather when midday temperatures get too high, butterflies seek shade, then become active again later in the day. This is particularly true in subtropical areas such as Ari-

A field of common milkweed in bloom can be a gold mine for the butterfly seeker.

How to Spot Butterflies

zona, Texas, and Florida, where they take an afternoon siesta.

Both during butterfly counts afield and in our own garden, we have noted that 9:00 A.M. till noon is usually by far the best for butterflying; afternoons are usually slower, with a resurgence in late afternoon. You will soon learn differences among groups. Monarchs, swallowtails, and anglewings are always the first to become active in the morning and remain active the latest in the afternoon. Correspondingly, they are often the only species active on cooler or cloudy days, when temperatures are in the 60s or 70s.

Skippers seem to require the most heat. A temperature over 80°F is generally needed for most (except for early springtime specialties such as Cobweb Skipper): 80°F with bright sun, 90°F without. Skippers nectar early in the day and can be more difficult to find midday to early afternoon. We once censused a lush milkweed patch around 9:00 A.M. and had more than 70 Rare Skippers. Revisiting the same field at 2:00 P.M., we had only three. Diversity was down too; the morning had produced ten species of skippers, the afternoon four. Midday they are patrolling territories, searching for mates, or ovipositing. Hairstreaks have a similar daily pattern, and it too is more behavioral than temperature induced. In a pine barrens forest, we once saw dozens of Striped Hairstreaks and Banded Hairstreaks in the morning, but saw only two a few hours later when returning by the same route. Hairstreaks show a marked pattern of early morning nectaring, followed by a midday retreat to

To find Striped Hairstreaks, learn their daily activity pattern.

the treetops. They are still active, but patrolling or awaiting mates, usually unseen by butterfly watchers far below.

An understanding of activity patterns and seasonality is important in butterfly spotting. Persistence rewards the watcher. Many times over the years, we have puzzled over a nectar patch devoid of butterflies, yet returned a few days later to find it abounding with butterflies. Geyata Ajilvsgi's excellent book, *Butterfly Gardening in the South*, explains how nectar production can be affected by temperature, wind, humidity, day length, sunlight, a plant's health, and how each plant's reaction to these conditions varies. Good nectar production often results from a cool night followed by a clear, hot day or mild, warm winds after rain. Strong, cold winds may shut down nectar production. The sun's warmth increases nectar production. So wildflowers and gardens in

Transmission-line right-of-ways can be excellent places to search for butterflies.

open, sunny spots offer the most nectar, and that nectar may become more abundant and more concentrated at midday.

Not only can a few degrees of temperature make a difference, but a few days can make a big difference in a butterfly's flight period — particularly for smaller, short-lived species. We have walked a woods road and seen one Brown Elfin and returned a week later to find more than a hundred. A seep-willow *(Baccharis)* patch at Box Canyon in southeastern Arizona yielded hundreds of butterflies one day, yet only a dozen four days later.

You will gradually learn the conditions that produce abundant butterflies in your area: various nectar source peaks, timing of flight periods, time of day, weather patterns, etc. Always remember that persistence pays off. An outing can have vastly different results with just a few degrees' change in tempera-

ture or when timed just an hour or two apart. In our own butterfly garden, we can find different species and varying numbers each time we check throughout the day. Therefore, visit and revisit good habitats and nectar patches throughout the day, and visit day after day, if possible. You will eventually be rewarded.

Where to Search for Butterflies

When we first focused on butterflies we thought we had to go somewhere special to see them, a butterfly watching spot or preserve. We soon learned, however, that the key to enjoying butterflies was as simple as picking a sunny day when butterflies were most active and following field edges, woods roads, trails, old railroad beds, or power lines, especially if these routes of easy access meandered through a variety of habitats. Most sites that are good for birds and birding are also excellent for butterflies and butterflying: natural areas, state and county parks, state and national forests, national wildlife refuges, national recreation areas, state wildlife management areas, reservations, wildlife sanctuaries, and Nature Conservancy preserves. Even if these properties were not preserved with butterflies in mind, butterflies benefit from all types of land preservation.

Explore a variety of habitats and you should discover a greater variety of butterflies, whether close to home or during travels. Each habitat type is home to unique plant communities and the butterflies dependent on those plants. See how many different habitats occur where you live or where you are traveling.

Learn to recognize and seek out dry deciduous and coniferous forests, edges of wet deciduous and coniferous swamp forests, bogs, hardwood hammocks, pine barren forests, pine barren sand hills, dune forests, meadows, pastures, river edges, stream edges, pond edges, freshwater marshes, saltmarsh edges, sawgrass prairies, desert waterholes, prairies, mesquite grasslands, tundra, high-elevation rocky slopes, and of course old fields and vacant lots to name a few.

Some species move a bit and might be in a nearby habitat taking advantage of a good nectar source. We've found Hessel's Hairstreaks on blooming sand myrtle along a dry, sandy pine barrens road, but always with a white-cedar swamp within view. Other species never leave their specialized habitat — Bog Coppers are always in acid bogs where cranberry grows. Search each habitat or likely areas nearby for good nectar sources and specific host plants of target species.

There are many regional butterfly books available for areas around the United States and Canada, and, with the increased interest in butterfly watching, others are being published at a rapid rate. Many of these regional books will alert you to good butterfly-watching spots and also offer excellent site-specific natural history information: local larval food-plants, nectar plants, flight period, and distribution.

Anyone lucky enough to live in the Northeast can benefit from the selected butterflying localities in Jeffrey Glassberg's book, *Butterflies Through Binoculars, A Field & Finding Guide to Butterflies in the Boston–New York–Washington Region*. Many of these sites are readily accessible public lands that support a great diversity and abundance of butterflies. Each site write-up also includes a butterfly checklist. *American Butterflies*, the quarterly journal of the North American Butterfly Association (NABA), includes "definitive destination" articles about butterfly-watching hotspots around the country. Each article shares excellent natural history information along with site-specific information about when and where to go and exactly which butterflies occur there. A site checklist accompanies each article.

Do not despair if your area is not covered by a regional butterfly book. Bird-finding books showcase natural areas that are birding hotspots, most of which are also excellent places for butterfly watching. As New Jersey residents we've used William Boyle's book, *A Guide to Bird Finding in New Jersey*, to explore the state, chapter by chapter, learning of out-of-the-way places with diverse habitats. The American Birding Association's sales catalog offers a complete list of regional birding guides (arranged state by state for the United States, province by province for Canada, and country by country for the rest of the world). These birdfinding guides are just as useful to butterfly watchers because they direct the reader to good habitats. We have used the popular Lane/ABA birdfinding guides to find excellent butterfly sites in Arizona, Florida, and Texas.

Butterfly gardens concentrate nectar and act as magnets to butterflies, especially if these gardens are near or include weedy areas and native trees, shrubs, and vines that are critical for egg laying. Formal gardens such as these can offer the watcher great looks and some of the best photographic opportunities. Perhaps there is a public butterfly garden in your area; there were more than 135 such gardens around the United States in 1993. With the interest in butterfly gardening there are no doubt many more now.

Migration hotspots like the Cape May peninsula concentrate not only birds but butterflies as well, migrants like Monarchs and vagrant species too. Lakeshores, river edges, peninsulas, and isthmuses all tend to concentrate butterflies on the move.

Search Techniques

While out for butterflies, walk slowly, staying alert for butterflies that you may flush in passing. Scan ahead with binoculars for nectar sources and check them to see if butterflies are present. Remember, many butterflies are tiny and easily overlooked. They can blend in with flowers, leaves, or even a sandy road surface and be quite inconspicuous. They may sit perfectly still, so don't count on movement to alert you to their presence. Move slowly around a stand of flowers, studying them with your binoculars, to see what may be hiding on the far side. Then go to the next nectar patch and repeat the process. Use the same technique to see puddling butterflies in wet areas such as puddles, seeps, rivulets, stream banks, pond edges, sandbars, and even damp, sandy road surfaces after a rain.

Butterfly gardens concentrate nectar and act as magnets to butterflies.

Once you spot a butterfly, move toward it low and slow. Their compound eyes easily detect movement. The simple act of pointing to a butterfly may flush it. Consider crouching down as you move toward a butterfly so that your shadow does not fall across it and flush it. Following these rules, you can usually approach until your binoculars will focus no closer. It's fun to inch in even closer, coming nose to antennae for a dazzling naked-eye look — close enough to see every scale! For close-up photos we often end up on our hands and knees. A pair of garden pants with padded knees works well for this approach.

If a butterfly does flush, don't despair. They frequently return to the same favorite nectar source or puddle edge. Perched butterflies overseeing their territory will very often return too. This seems particularly true with skippers, but hairstreaks and brushfoots will do this too, especially if they are hilltopping or treetopping. In each case, focus your binoculars on the spot and be ready for their return.

Although open paths and trails are usually best, there are times when you need to go off-road. The best butterfly spotters don't mind bushwhacking, going off trails into dense fields or brush. In this way, you can find flowering plants you might otherwise overlook, or actually flush out butterflies hunkered down in the grass, roosting or resting. Many butterflies are discovered as they flush ahead, and frequently they fly only a short distance and perch again. Watch where they land, then approach slowly. Bushwhacking, however, is not always an option. Many nature reserves and parks ask visitors to stay on trails in order to protect fragile vegetation. In these areas, follow the rules! Whenever you are out butterfly watching avoid crushing vegetation, especially nectar sources and host plants. We watched one photographer who was a proverbial bull in a china shop, flattening milkweed every time he turned around. Tread lightly, watching where you step.

At times you need to tap bushes and trees to find butterflies. We often carry a walking stick for just this purpose. Hairstreaks, elfins, and other species may retire to treetops at some point in the day; if you are in likely habitat and do not see target species, try tapping the host plant or likely nectar sources. Pine Elfins, so elusive for years, became quite common once we learned to gently tap young pine trees. Seeing an 'Olive' Juniper Hairstreak may be as simple as tapping or gently shaking a young redcedar tree. We saw our first Hessel's Hairstreak by exploring edges of white cedar swamps and tapping likely looking nectar sources. They blended in so well with the pink, cream, and green bell-shaped flowers of black huckleberry that we never would have seen them otherwise.

Spotting a flushed butterfly and following it with your naked eye is a learned technique, more art than science. Even for veterans, swirling hairstreaks or skippers often escape into thin air right before the eyes. Some people spot flushed butterflies far better than others. Practice makes perfect, and good spotters have probably spent many, many hours afield enjoying elusive butterflies. You might be able to follow large butterflies with your binoculars. If they pitch down a short distance away, mark the spot by picking out a landmark, then hike toward it, scanning ahead as you go. A butterfly's shadow may catch your attention; look toward the sun to find it. Be alert for all clues.

Wind can be a factor as you try to follow flushed butterflies. A calm day makes it easy, while blustery winds make it almost impossible as the butterfly whips out of sight. On windy days, particularly in spring and fall when temperatures might be marginal, butterflies seek protected spots out of the wind. So look for sunny spots, in a lee, out of brisk winds.

In quiet conditions, our friend Jim Dowdell identified a butterfly by sound. No, not by "call"; butterflies make no vocal sounds, but the wings of some make considerable noise as they fly. A butterfly dashed past and disappeared. Jim called out, "Silver-spotted Skipper." "How could you tell?" we asked. "By the sound," he replied. We've since noted their distinctive dry rattle in flight. Crackers are also noisy, named for the sharp snapping sound heard when they fly.

When searching a large area during butterfly census efforts or 4th of July Butterfly Counts, we will crisscross likely habitats, sometimes separating to cover parallel transects. When woods roads or trails transect good habitats we often explore by bicycle. We've found that we see more than we would if traveling by car, and we can stop, look, and scan more quickly and easily. We have sought butterflies by bicycle during NABA 4th of July Butterfly Counts in the New Jersey pine barrens and during winter vacations in the vast Florida Everglades. We have one friend who loves butterflying by horse.

Consider canoes and kayaks, too, as a means of getting into otherwise hard to view or reach habitats where butterflies might be. Our first Great Purple Hairstreaks in the East were discovered during a canoe trip through a cypress swamp in coastal South Carolina. We spotted the first one on the white flowers of climbing hempweed. After that, we paddled ahead to each stretch where this vine flourished and were rewarded with more hairstreaks and other butterflies too.

Search for Unsavory Delights

When searching for butterflies, put to use what you know about butterfly behavior. Always be alert for puddles, animal droppings, animal carcasses, rotting fruit, and sap flows. Each, in its own way, attracts butterflies. After spring and summer rain showers explore sandy roads for puddling butterflies. If you encounter butterflies puddling at a dry area, it may mean an animal has urinated there, and the butterfly is getting minerals from the spot. On a hot summer day a butterfly may even land on your perspiration-dampened arm. They land to drink the moisture and obtain salts.

Unsavory delights such as animal droppings, animal carcasses, rotting fruit, and

Common Alpines and a Hoffmann's Checkerspot get salts from bear scat *(above)*. **Overripe fruit attracts butterflies such as this Question Mark** *(right)*.

flowing sap are preferred over flower nectar by Red Admirals, White Admirals, Red-spotted Purples, and most anglewings, leafwings, emperors, and wood nymphs. They obtain moisture and nutrients from animal droppings, or scat — whether dog droppings in a yard, bear scat in the woods, horse manure on a trail, or cow manure in a pasture. Bird droppings, when fresh and damp, will attract some butterflies too. One of our best looks at a tiny Harvester was of one perched on a huge rock in the center of a stream. It was totally preoccupied with a fresh bird dropping as a dozen of us inched in for close-up looks. At Ramsey Canyon in southeastern Arizona we had a similar encounter with a California Sister. It was so busy feeding on a bird dropping on a streamside rock that we got within inches of it. You may not want to scout for scat, but when you come across it be alert for butterflies. The same holds true for animal carcasses. The putrid flesh offers up moisture and nutrients to certain butterflies.

Be alert for sap flows due to an injury, a broken limb, or freshly drilled Yellow-bellied Sapsucker holes. Make a mental note of such spots and return often. You'll nearly always be rewarded. Sometimes year after year the same tree sports a sap seep. We know of one gnarled old wild cherry that is guaranteed to give good looks at Red Admirals, Question Marks, and Eastern Commas, often all drinking together.

An abandoned orchard or even a single tree with overripe, rotting fruit left on the ground is a real find for the butterfly spotter. Errant banana peels, apple cores, and watermelon rinds will also attract butterflies. Don't neces-

sarily look for them, but check all you see!

A colleague, Dale Schweitzer, often baits for butterflies on a 4th of July Butterfly Count in southern New Jersey, usually tallying the only Hackberry Emperors and Tawny Emperors of the day. His method? In the vicinity of hackberry trees, their host plant, he paints trees with a specially prepared sweet glop early in the morning, then checks the spot several times throughout the day to see what species have been attracted. This is a well-known method for scientific Lepidoptera census efforts, but it can work for the recreational butterflier as well. Often called "sugaring," the prepared glop is a great butterfly attractor for those species that commonly feed on rotting fruit. Butterflies have an excellent sense of smell and may be attracted over long distances. Baiting butterflies like this concentrates them from a large area, making your search easier. At night moths will be drawn in too. Don't be disappointed if your efforts seem to fail; no butterfly feeds constantly. Butterflies spend quite a bit of time perched near good feeding sites. Return to the bait again and again, and explore the area nearby to see what you may flush.

One word of caution: put the bait concoction on older trees with ridged or furrowed bark, not on young or thin-barked trees. Over time it may stain the tree, which does no harm, but squirrels gnawing on the tree where bait is placed will injure a young or thin-barked tree.

Butterfly bait is simple to make. With molasses as the base, mix in ripe bananas or other rotting fruit and enough beer to make it spreadable. Store, covered, for a few days before using. Choose a route through both sunny and shady locations since many brushfoots seek shade at midday. Then paint a patch of bait onto selected trees along the route. Since it is easy to lose track of which trees you baited and inadvertently flush butterflies while walking the bait trail, somehow mark each baited tree so you know exactly where to look upon your return.

There are several other wacky ways to attract butterflies to you. If you are in an area with little to concentrate butterflies, yet see patrolling individuals, try propping up a swatch of bright red cloth — some butterflies may come in to investigate. We know of one person who has had success by simply placing a red soda can on a stick. Taking this a step further, we know one professional lepidopterist who, when faced with doing a survey in an area with few flowers, carries in lush, flowering potted plants, then checks them for nectaring butterflies from time to time through the day.

Butterflies may also investigate bright clothing. Fritillaries seem to key in on yellow. A yellow slicker spread in a field has been known to attract passing, patrolling fritillaries. One butterfly enthusiast stops patrolling fritillaries for identification and enjoyment by tossing an orange, or piece of orange, into its path as it goes by. The male, the one that usually patrols, will then pounce on the orange, thinking it either a potential mate or an adversary. This also reportedly works on Ruddy Daggerwings, which have a proclivity to perch high up in trees where they are hard to see. If you sight one and desire a better look, toss an orange object up into the air by the butterfly (fishing floats are said to work well). The so challenged male will follow the object to the ground, affording good looks.

Canvassing for Caterpillars

Another highly specialized form of finding butterflies is to search for them in an earlier life stage: egg, caterpillar, or chrysalis. Two books we consider essential for this endeavor are Paul Opler's "big book," *Butterflies East of the Great Plains,* and James Scott's *The Butterflies of North America.* Each gives detailed natural history information hard to find elsewhere about eggs, caterpillars, chrysalids, life cycle timing, and host plants.

When you find a caterpillar on a plant or a butterfly laying eggs on a plant and you identify the plant, you then want to know which butterfly (or moth) uses it as a host plant. For this reason any butterfly field guide that includes an index to host plants is invaluable; regional guides are especially helpful. Amy Wright's excellent *Peterson First Guide to Caterpillars* is a wonderful introduction to many of the most common butterfly and moth caterpillars. Some butterfly books, such as Thomas Allen's *The Butterflies of West Virginia and Their Caterpillars,* illustrate the caterpillar stage. Half the battle is knowing what you are looking for, fine-tuning a search image. With the publication of such books more and more tools are available to those willing to learn.

Finding butterflies before they become butterflies is not for everyone. It requires a keen eye and diligent searching. We know several butterfly spotters who greatly enjoy it. During a recent NABA 4th of July Butterfly Count in coastal South Carolina, Freddy Arthur seemed to find as many butterfly caterpillars as we did adult butterflies. Freddy owns and maintains a live butterfly exhibit, the Butterfly Barn, in McClellanville; she is intimately familiar with the host plants for each local species and has developed an incredible search image to find tiny caterpillars on plants.

Seeing an adult butterfly repeatedly touch down on nonflowering plants is a good clue that she is laying eggs. Watch closely with your binoculars. When the butterfly wanders off, step in and try to find the very, very tiny eggs, which are often laid singly. Identify the plant with the proper field guide (wildflower guide; tree, shrub, and vine guide; or grasses guide). Look up the butterfly's host plant or plants to see if there is a match. In just this way we learned that Red-spotted Purples lay their many-faceted eggs on the pointed tips of wild cherry leaves.

Red-spotted Purples lay a single egg on the very tip of a wild cherry leaf.

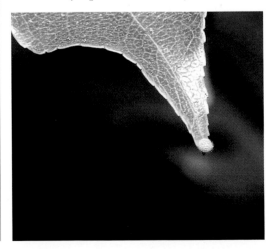

Most caterpillars do not feed out in the open; they have too many predators. To avoid predators some caterpillars look like bird droppings, others hide in the curled edge of a leaf, some are covered with nasty spines, and many are so cryptically marked and colored that they look exactly like the flower bud, leaf, or pine needle they are feeding on. Jane Ruffin once showed us a tiny Spring Azure caterpillar feeding on a small green developing blueberry

on a highbush blueberry shrub. It took her quite a while to initially find it. Even once discovered, it took us ages to rediscover it each time we looked away.

One clue to finding caterpillars is to look for frass, or caterpillar droppings. These are a dead giveaway, lying below the feeding caterpillar. Often though, you will find the "poops" without finding the caterpillar, which means it has moved on to another leaf or plant or that it has been discovered and eaten. Look for chewed leaves to follow its trail — many will have been munched by beetles, aphids, or other bugs, but you will soon learn

what caterpillar-chewed leaves look like.

Also learn to recognize caterpillar houses. Some caterpillars web leaves or flower parts together, creating hidden rooms on their host plant. Painted Lady caterpillars web together thistle leaves. The silvery undersides of the leaves stand out and the alert observer quickly learns to spot these caterpillar hideouts. Red Admiral caterpillars web together nettle leaves. The already furry flower heads of pearly everlasting look even fluffier when webbed together by American Lady caterpillars. You can gently tease open a caterpillar house and take a peek at the caterpillar inside. Be sure to reclose it, leaving it as you found it, so that the caterpillar remains safe from predators.

The Red-spotted Purple winters over as a partially grown caterpillar, surviving the winter in its hibernaculum — a wild cherry leaf that it silked shut and attached to the branch the previous fall so it would remain on the tree when the other leaves dropped. As wild cherry trees leaf out in the spring, Red-spotted Purple caterpillars venture out and begin to eat and grow again. In winter it is always a treat when we notice a bare wild cherry tree with a lone leaf hanging — a silked-shut leaf with a treasure inside.

Many gardeners have discovered large green caterpillars with black bands and yellow spots happily munching their parsley, dill, fennel, rue, celery, or carrot plants. One can

Some caterpillars, such as this American Lady caterpillar *(left)*, web leaves together. Frass, or caterpillar droppings, alert one to feeding caterpillars, such as Monarch *(right)*.

A Black Swallowtail nursery of caterpillars feeding on fresh dill can be educational in a classroom or home setting.

only hope that a knowledgeable friend enlightened them: "Oh yes, leave it alone — it becomes the lovely Black Swallowtail butterfly." Some adventuresome folks even bring the caterpillars indoors and set up a feeding chamber, supplying them with precious parsley, dill, or fennel. The tricky time comes when one last butterfly has not emerged and the chrysalis is left as winter approaches. This chrysalis is not a dead thing at all, but the form in which the Black Swallowtail winters over. Take it out of your warm house and place it in an outbuilding for the winter so it does not get tricked into thinking spring is here before spring actually comes. Be sure to mist it oc-

casionally with a plant mister as nature does with rain or snow showers. Keep an eye on it as temperatures warm so that you can release the first Black Swallowtail of spring!

Finding a tiny caterpillar, bringing it home, setting up an empty aquarium with a screened top for it, rearing it on cuttings from its host plant until it enters the chrysalis stage, watching the adult butterfly emerge from the chrysalis, then releasing the butterfly back to the wild can be a priceless experience for any child or adult. It can also be a full-time hobby when done on a scale larger than one or two caterpillars. Rearing five or six Monarch caterpillars alone means a daily mission to replenish their milkweed food supply. Fail to feed them and they will die. Fail to clean up after them and they may die. Be sure to give them a suitable perch for the chrysalis to attach to — a stick leaning across the chamber works fine. Give them enough room to spread their wings when they emerge from the chrysalis or they may dry with a rumpled wing and be unable to fly. Be sure to read Robert Pyle's *Handbook for Butterfly Watchers* and Paul Opler's *Peterson Field Guide to Eastern Butterflies* for thorough discussions of how to raise butterflies.

Spotting eggs, caterpillars, and chrysalids is the ultimate challenge in butterflying, a real specialty. You can learn a great deal about butterflies this way. A walk outdoors will never be the same once you've begun to focus on the other butterfly life stages.

Butterfly Identification

Identification skills are as much a part of butterfly watching as they are of bird watching. Once you have spotted a butterfly, take note of its size, shape, color pattern, and even behavior and habitat. Beginners focus primarily on the size, general colors, and overall patterns. Over time butterfliers begin to also notice the subtle differences in shapes and tones of similarly appearing species and also learn to distinguish flight patterns. For instance, a skipper flies differently from a satyr. A Viceroy flies more quickly and directly than a Monarch, the species it mimics in color and pattern.

Begin testing your identification skills with the large showy butterflies. Gradually work down to the tiny and easily overlooked butterflies. Save the skippers for last, since they are the hardest and the most frustrating to identify. One wag has suggested that they are so named because you "skip" them rather than belabor their identification. Skippers are the "little brown jobs" of the butterfly world. Many people never totally master the intricacies of variations in pattern and the effects of worn scales in some skippers. The best butterfliers we know will admit, every so often, "I'm not sure," when confronted with a nondescript and usually worn skipper.

We are fortunate to have a number of excellent field guides that make identification fun rather than frustrating. In the past, butterfly enthusiasts had to use nets, kill the butterfly, and then compare it to illustrations of pinned specimens in field guides to make difficult identifications. Today, a number of field guides are instead being illustrated with butterflies in lifelike poses so they can be compared with the watcher's view through binoculars. We've never been partial to photographic bird field guides, never felt they were as good as guides illustrated with composite paintings of live birds. For butterfly identification, we feel the opposite is true. Robert Michael Pyle's *The Audubon Society Field Guide to North American Butterflies* was a landmark book in that it used photos of live butterflies in natural settings. Previous guides, although certainly adding to our body of knowledge, used photographs or paintings of pinned butterflies. This particularly did not help with identification of many of the blues, hairstreaks, satyrs, and folded-winged skippers, most of which nearly always perch with

Skippers, such as this Swarthy Skipper, can be the hardest butterflies to identify.

their wings closed or folded. Pyle's book was a turning point for butterfly watching. Jeffrey Glassberg's *Butterflies Through Binoculars* took this concept one step further.

In Glassberg's *Butterflies Through Binoculars* books, photos depict similar butterflies in similar poses, from similar angles, and they are sized to be in scale with one another. For the traveling butterfly watcher, Pyle and Glassberg are essentials. In the East you still need Paul Opler's *Peterson Field Guide to Eastern Butterflies* for in-depth natural history information and range maps. Out West many refer to James Scott's *The Butterflies of North America* for in-depth information and range maps. New books are coming out all the time, including Paul Opler's *Peterson Field Guide to Western Butterflies* and others in the Butterflies Through Binoculars series, so butterfly identification will get easier and easier.

With more than 700 species known in North America, good range maps and regional field guides help make butterfly identification manageable. When paging through a field guide, make sure the butterfly you've tentatively identified is found in your area. For example, Two-tailed Swallowtail appears very similar to the Eastern Tiger Swallowtail, yet the Two-tailed is exclusively a westerner and the Eastern Tiger is an avowed easterner, with virtually no overlap.

To make our field guide more user friendly during travels, we've learned to annotate it. Before a trip to, say, the Canadian Maritimes, we use the range maps in either Opler or Scott to determine which species we are likely to encounter. We then mark up our field guide with colored dots (available from office supply stores) next to the illustration or photo and accompanying text of those species we may see. After a number of trips and annotations a key is necessary: Orange = Canadian Maritime; Blue = South Florida, etc. This is, first of all, good research and preparation for any trip, but it is also a tremendous help in the field. If a confusing fritillary is seen, for example, you

How to Spot Butterflies

can eliminate many of the noncontenders by focusing on the likely ones (those with dots) and ignore look-alikes that simply aren't found there.

When available, butterfly checklists are an invaluable guide to butterfly identification, listing the species occurring in a given area and the seasonality and status of each. This is more than half the battle in butterfly identification — knowing what to look for when. The "definitive destination" articles in NABA's journal, *American Butterflies,* are one of the best sources of butterfly checklists. In addition, some excellent regional checklists have been published by butterfly clubs, bird observatories, and individuals and are available at national and state parks and nature centers. Checklists based on a long-standing history of butterfly study in a particular area are highly accurate and useful. An excellent example is "A Distributional Checklist of the Butterflies and Skippers of the New York City Area (50-mile Radius) and Long Island," edited by Rick Cech, published by the New York City Butterfly Club. It is based on club records from 1985 through 1992 and historical records. The checklist uses bar graphs to show flight periods and expected numbers, and it also lists 51 selected butterfly-watching sites in the area. Another example of an annotated checklist is the "Butterflies of Greater Los Angeles," published by the Center for the Conservation of Biodiversity/Lepidoptera Research Foundation. This full-color brochure includes illustrations and detailed regional information for each species.

Though they're not yet as readily available as bird checklists, ask for butterfly checklists whenever you visit national and state parks and nature centers — create the demand.

One butterfly identification activity we have had fun with is butterfly cards — a collection of butterfly wings mounted on annotated index cards. None was killed by us; we refuse to collect live butterflies under any circumstance, feeling that for recreational purposes our cameras can adequately record even the hardest to identify. All were either road kills, found on road shoulders; spider kills, found in spider webs; or dead butterflies found on truck or car grills. Automobiles are by far the top butterfly predator in all but the most remote areas of the country. We have been picking up road-kill butterflies for years. You will be surprised how many you will find if you look for them. During roadside walks, hikes, and bicycle rides we invariably find a dead butterfly or two. While some are smashed, many are in remarkably good shape. Never try to collect from heavily traveled roads — it is too dangerous. Lightly traveled roads are best; fewer butterflies may be found, but they are often in better shape. It may seem amazing that in just ten years of mounting road kills, we now have a teaching collection of about 75 percent of the species commonly found in Cape May County.

When we come across a road-kill butterfly, we drop it into a pocket container, such as an empty Band-Aid box, and take it home. Then we cut the wings off with an exacto knife and use clear tape to attach the wings to a 3" × 5" note card. We record the species, location, date, and sex, if known, in the upper corner or on the back. Then we place the butterfly's right set of wings with the upperside (dorsal) showing on the right side of the card and the butterfly's left set of wings with the underside (ventral) showing on the left side of the card — for easy comparisons between individuals of the same species and different species. (Putting a tiny drop of Elmer's glue on the card as the wing is placed keeps it from jumping up to the tape because of static electricity.)

These cards can be used as flash cards to learn identification points or as educational tools. The cards have been especially useful to show variability in size and patterns. Some individual butterflies are runts, often as a result of a problem with the host plant (drought, flood, cutting) while in the caterpillar stage. The caterpillar pupates early, before full size, and the butterfly that emerges is smaller than normal. Putting cards side by side readily shows variations like these. Since only wings and no body parts are taped to the cards, they last for years. It's fun to have a collection that you didn't kill to collect.

Lists and Record Keeping

Another fun aspect of butterfly watching is butterfly listing. Just as many birders keep a life list, butterfly watchers are now doing the same, recording the details of the first time they see each new species. Our butterfly records at first consisted of simple check marks in our field guides along with annotations of the dates and places encountered. As we became more aware, we began also noting host and nectar plants we saw butterflies using. Now, in preparation for trips, we go to

great lengths to prepare a butterfly checklist of what is possible in the area.

There is still so much to learn about butterflies. Careful records and detailed notes may have true scientific value and contribute to the understanding of a region's butterflies. Every butterfly checklist ever published is based on field notes of individual naturalists; noted flight periods have their basis in the daily records of people afield. Records of dates of early- and late-season sightings are crucial to the big picture and help sort out differences region by region.

Some people even keep track of the number of species they've seen in their yards, a yard list. In New Jersey, a friendly competition among butterfly gardeners has evolved to see who can attract the most species over time. Yard lists are usually cumulative — how many butterfly species you have recorded on your property over time. In 20 years we've seen 70 species in our garden in Goshen, New Jersey, but Jim and Deb Dowdell, ten miles farther south, are gaining fast with 51 species in just three years since they began their garden. Our yard checklist hangs on the refrigerator, and it's a proud day when a new species is checked off. It takes a *really* rare immigrant for a new check on our yard list, but we can always hope!

Birding big days, in which you search for the most species you can possibly record in a state in a 24-hour period, have triggered butterflying big days, a true test of knowledge of butterfly distribution, habitat needs, flight periods, and identification. NABA 4th of July Butterfly Counts are like big days. There is a friendly competition between count circles and a rivalry for high count each year. We approach butterfly counts somewhat like a big day, planning our route carefully. "Let's see, to get Bog Copper we need to hit Head-of-River Bog, and while we're there, it's a short way over to Tarkiln Bog for the Black Dash colony. Oh yeah, while we're up there, the fields in Peaslee WMA are our best bet for Great Spangled Fritillary. Maybe, with luck, we can find an early individual of the second brood of Peck's Skipper."

A few statewide butterfly big days have been done and are the ultimate test of one's knowledge of distribution and occurrence, not to mention observer stamina. A game, yes, pure fun to some, silly to others. But, if we can have Bird-A-Thon big days, in which pledges per species raise money for conservation, why not a "Butterfly-A-Thon" to raise money for much-needed Lepidoptera conservation?

Record keeping can be done in many ways. We still use a cumbersome old-fashioned system of notebooks and file folders, each labeled for a favorite area or place we've traveled to. The best organizational tool for record keeping of various life, year, yard, and photograph lists is the *NABA Checklist & English Names of North American Butterflies,* published in 1995. This checklist includes the Latin name and standardized English names for all 717 species recorded in North America north of Mexico.

Just as in birding, computers have revolutionized butterfly record keeping. We have friends who keep their butterfly journal records on *LepiList,* software that contains the NABA checklist mentioned above and allows for many types of listing and data management (see Further Information).

Remember, your sightings may be the basis for increased knowledge. There is still so much to learn and so much to be understood. Whether out locally or on vacation in the Arctic tundra, keep detailed notes and you may contribute significantly to known information.

Learn from the Experts

As with so many natural history disciplines, you can greatly accelerate the learning process by spending time with experts. Local chapters of the North American Butterfly Association and an increasing number of nature centers, nature clubs, bird clubs, and bird observatories offer organized butterfly walks. If you are new to butterflying, seek them out. These walks teach participants how to look for butterflies and how to find good habitats. Attend butterfly walks as frequently as possible since you're likely to see and learn about new species and different places each time.

The North American Butterfly Association (NABA), founded in 1992, already had 3,000 members and 15 local chapters by its sixth year. The chapters are scattered around the United States and offer regular field trips, meetings and programs, and a way to meet fellow butterfly watchers in your area and share information about butterfly identification, photography, gardening, and more. If there is a NABA chapter near you, take advantage of it.

NABA publications *(American Butterflies, Butterfly Garden News, Annual Report of NABA 4th of July Butterfly Counts)* abound with learning opportunities. Articles by experts from around the country cover identification, photography, hotspots, and gardening and conservation issues.

NABA's first three Biennial Members' Meetings were held at peak times for butterfly diversity and at sites famous for specialty butterflies (New Jersey pine barrens in 1994, southeastern Arizona in 1996, and the high plains of Colorado in 1998). Each meeting attracted participants from all over the United States, Canada, Great Britain, and Mexico and brought together many knowledgeable leaders. Meetings combined field trips and workshops, enabling participants to see and learn a great deal in a short period.

More than 330 NABA 4th of July Butterfly Counts are held each summer in the United States, Canada, and Mexico. There is undoubtedly one held near where you live. (See Further Information for full details on NABA.)

New Jersey Audubon Society's Cape May Bird Observatory (CMBO) has offered numerous butterfly-watching opportunities since 1989, including weekly butterfly walks spring through fall and wildlife habitat workshops with a strong emphasis on gardening for butterflies and hummingbirds. CMBO's butterfly map, checklist, and hotline all combine to make the Cape May area very butterfly watcher–friendly.

The Southeastern Arizona Bird Observatory (SABO) offers spring and summer walks at local natural areas and workshops on wildlife-friendly gardening. SABO's Living

Take advantage of every learning opportunity, such as butterfly walks and outings. Here Bob Pyle leads a NABA field trip in Colorado.

Jewels workshop in August highlights butterflies, hummingbirds, and wildflowers. (See Further Information for further details on CMBO and SABO.)

A few private tour companies offer butterfly-specific tours. Jeffrey Glassberg's Butterflies Through Binoculars Tours to butterfly-watching hotspots throughout the country offer excellent learning experiences. Victor Emanuel Nature Tours offers an annual trip to the Monarch overwintering sites in Mexico. Organized tours depend heavily on scouting beforehand and making contacts with local butterfliers. Leaders on such tours are knowledgeable and experienced butterfliers and naturalists.

Butterfly Watching Group Etiquette

When we lead butterfly walks we do not use a net but instead encourage participants to use binoculars. We find that people get much more involved if they use binoculars and learn how to look for and find butterflies themselves, a skill they can take home. By using binoculars rather than nets, participants are able to study butterflies in their natural setting, learn how camouflaged they can be and how unusual some of their behaviors are, learn which flowers they favor (many of which first-time butterfly watchers had previously lumped into the worthless-weed category), and much more.

Too often a net in the hands of a leader results in participants becoming less and less involved, idly waiting for the leader to net the next butterfly, pop it into a jar, and pass it around. After it is released, boredom sets in until the next butterfly is captured. On our walks we instead invite participants to help us find butterflies. With so many eyes looking we're never skunked, even in bad weather. Many butterflies are discovered as they flush ahead of the group, but quite often someone in the back spots a butterfly flushed by those in the front. Frequently our quarry flies only a short distance and perches again on a tree limb or leaves right next to the path or in the path itself.

A quick explanation of how to point out a butterfly saves a great deal of frustration later on. We'll often do it with the first or second butterfly of the walk. We first find a prominent landmark near the butterfly. Then, once everyone is keyed into this landmark, we'll explain where the butterfly is in relation to it. For example, "Stop! There's a butterfly ahead. See the second tree shadow that crosses our path? Look with your binoculars at the flat stone on the far side of that shadow. The butterfly is just beyond the stone. See it? It's facing us." We make sure to ask if everyone sees it. If the majority of the group is still floundering, we pick a different set of obvious landmarks. There may be a few viewers who still can't find it. One trick is to use the shadow of a finger to point at the butterfly, telling folks where it is in relation to the finger's shadow. A walking stick makes shadow pointing easy. And we always remind people to move slowly — any quick movement and the butterfly will flush.

Everyone will get a good look if the group has been properly briefed on butterflying etiquette first: 1) stop collectively when a butterfly is spotted; 2) let everyone get a look, even if distant, before anyone in the group moves forward and inadvertently flushes the butterfly; 3) once the group has gotten a look and everyone knows where it is, move slowly ahead and stop again collectively to get a closer look; 4) once everyone has had a satisfactory look, single observers who want a naked-eye look or photographers can crouch down and approach slowly and low, being very careful not to let their shadow pass over the butterfly, and also being careful to back away in a similar fashion so that the next observer can also enjoy the butterfly; and 5) do not trample plants or gardens for any reason — even for a photograph. Such actions reflect poorly on all butterfly watchers.

Through the Seasons

MARCH HAS NEVER BEEN our favorite month, with frequent rain and cold winds off the winter-chilled Atlantic. In fact, inland areas green up weeks before the seaside town of Cape May. March is a month when we desperately await the warmth and green of spring.

From spring (Spring Azure in February, *above*) through fall (migrating Monarchs gathered on sedum in late September, *right*) butterflies complement each and every outing.

A cold front had passed two days before, and despite frost each night, the morning dawned with a warm, surging southerly breeze, a respite. It was the kind of day when you can almost *smell* spring. Rationalizing that our English Setter needed a run, deadlines and unreturned phone calls were pushed to the back of the desk. It was time for a walk.

A short drive took us to Belleplain State Forest. As we passed the bank in Dennisville, the temperature read 54°F, the date March 21. We parked at the head of Old Robbins Trail, a little used and mostly forgotten gravel road.

As we walked through the forest, Pine Warblers warbled overhead, and a din of Wood Frogs could be heard from the wet swamp behind a white cedar stand. A few Spring Peepers tried to show enthusiasm, but were fairly hoarse after their long winter sleep and sounded like they needed to be tuned. We were hopeful. It was maybe *just* warm enough in the sun and out of the wind for this to be *the* day. Not too long ago the first Osprey "made" the spring, but in recent years we've searched for something

more — in fact something very small and slight.

The dog flushed it first. A Spring Azure, the first butterfly of spring — flashing iridescent blue, sparkling, alive. Joined by another, they engaged in a swirling, spiraling courtship flight then returned to puddling in the wet gravel of the road. Magically the drab and brown winter forest was transposed. Somehow these thumbnail-sized flashes of color had energized the whole woodland. The greens of the pitch pines were greener, the browns of the oak leaves richer, the grays and greens of the lichens softer. This butterfly's life cycle was beginning anew, and just as suddenly for us winter had ended and the butterfly season had finally begun.

The next mile yielded perhaps eight Spring Azures, a few of each of the forms, *lucia* and *marginata.* The confused species concept of this group was forgotten as we watched the frenzied chases, the blue uppersides glistening in the warm sun. Then, overhead, on patrol, was another butterfly — a Question Mark! It swirled about, even capturing the interest of our dog. Finally it settled on a pine and spread its wings to absorb sunlight and warmth, and we saw the rich purple edge to the orange on the upper surface. This indicated, as expected, that this anglewing was from last fall's brood. The Spring Azures had just emerged as adult butterflies from their overwintering chrysalis stage, but this Question Mark had survived the winter in hibernation as an adult butterfly — concealed and insulated within a hollow tree or some other safe haven. Now it was patrolling the road searching for a mate. Spring!

A large dark butterfly sailed by and landed on a fallen branch — a Mourning Cloak. Burnt umber edged in soft yellow, with tiny bright blue spots. We wondered if this perfect Mourning Cloak, unlike the somewhat worn Question Mark, was possibly a new arrival from the South as opposed to an overwintering individual. It was an intriguing thought that our three species of butterflies represented three distinct "life styles": freshly emerged Spring Azures, overwintered Question Marks (born in the fall), and a possible migrant Mourning Cloak returning from the South.

Our afternoon outing had been a race against time. As we rounded up the dog and returned to the car, an advancing high band of clouds had already obscured the sun and a chill had descended. Another slow-moving cold front would bring back winter and delay spring's progress for a few more days or even a week or two.

On the way home the bank's sign read 49°F. No more butterflying today. But that didn't matter. Forget the singing robins, forget the green and lush skunk cabbage, forget the newly arrived Laughing Gulls clamoring yesterday. Even if brief, today's encounter broke winter's spell. It was spring and it couldn't be denied! We had seen our first butterflies of the season.

Throughout North America we all await the appearance of butterflies after their lengthy winter absence. Only in south Florida, south Texas, southern California, and Mexico can watchers enjoy adult butterflies on the wing all year long. Temperatures need to be 55° to 60°F or higher for them to fly, so wet and cold winters can put a damper on butterfly activity and butterfly watching even in these areas of year-round activity. Butterfly seasons are lengthiest in tropical areas and get briefer the farther north one goes or the higher the elevation. In the Arctic tundra the butterfly season lasts a brief but intense two months, from mid-June to mid-August. Between Florida and the Arctic, in the Mid-Atlantic states, the butterfly season generally begins once nights of freezing temperatures are past, in March or April, and continues until nights of freezing temperatures occur again, in October or November.

The First Butterflies of Spring

Perhaps Robert Frost said it best in his poem "Two Tramps in Mud Time":

The sun was warm but the wind was chill.
You know how it is with an April day
When the sun is out and the wind is still,
You're one month on in the middle of May.
But if you so much as dare to speak,
A cloud comes over the sunlit arch,
A wind comes off a frozen peak,
And you're two months back in the middle
   of March.

Once you have caught the butterfly-watching bug, spring seems to take forever to evolve. Butterflies' dependence on solar-powered activity is most evident during the changing weather of spring. Cool, cloudy days can make butterfly finding amazingly difficult, if not impossible, and we tend to go afield for butterflies only on warm spring days.

On such days, however, the rewards can be great. A stretch of warm days and nights above freezing anywhere from late February through March may produce the first butterflies of spring in southern New Jersey. They reappear from so many places. Species that overwintered as adults in hibernation tucked safely under a piece of bark or down in a hollow tree awaken and begin to explore, looking for sap flows or wet sandy surfaces. The first lengthy stretch of warm weather forces many plants to bud and triggers the emergence of Spring Azures that overwintered in the chrysalis stage in the leaf litter at the base of their host plant. If the weather holds and spring truly rushes forward, other spring specialties will emerge in force and begin to fly, such as the various elfins, Falcate Orangetip, Juvenal's Duskywing, Sleepy Duskywing, and Cobweb Skipper — single-brooded butterflies with only one spring flight. The *only* time to see them is during this brief appearance.

One of our most amazing spring butterflies is the Spring Azure. It is commonly believed that adults live only four days at the most, sometimes less. Typically a female emerges and mates the same day, lays eggs the second day, and dies. Luckily for watchers, the timing of the brood is protracted with successive emergences of adults, and Spring Azures can be enjoyed for more than a month — just not the same individuals. Continued research may prove Spring Azures to be longer lived than generally assumed. Several researchers feel they may be hardier than previously believed.

Spring quests for elfins depend entirely on looking for their specific host plant since they are very localized and do not migrate or travel any distance. Host plants may vary from region to region. In New Jersey, Brown Elfins are widespread since they lay eggs on blueberry, while Henry's Elfins can be harder to find since they need holly for egg laying. Frosted Elfin can be tough, as it needs wild indigo or sometimes lupine. Eastern Pine Elfin is widespread like its host plants, pines. Hoary Elfin is very localized and found *only* in sandy pine barrens where bearberry, its larval foodplant, grows.

Spring butterfly watching is at its peak in April and May in most of the East. Species that overwintered locally as adults, such as Red Admiral, Question Mark, Eastern Comma, and Mourning Cloak, are readily found, plus a number of species begin to emerge that might be found throughout the summer, such as Cabbage White, Orange Sulphur, and Clouded Sulphur. All will combine to stretch your daily list. By late April and early May other summer butterflies begin to emerge — not yet dozens, but one or two of each: Eastern Tiger Swallowtail, Spicebush Swallowtail, Eastern Tailed Blue, Pearl Crescent, American Copper, Gray Hairstreak, 'Olive' Juniper Hairstreak, and Red-banded Hairstreak. Now, too, new arrivals from the South appear, species that cannot survive northern winters in any form, but return each spring to repopulate: Monarch, American Lady, and Painted Lady.

Some years we are much too eager to wait for spring. We've left winter behind in New Jersey and taken trips south seeking spring and spring butterflies. In coastal South Carolina we have enjoyed Falcate Orangetips nectaring on dewberry and Juvenal's Duskywings on blueberry at the end of March. In fact by April 7, if the weather cooperates, butterfly diversity in South Carolina can be like an early summer day in New Jersey. During a late-winter visit to southeastern Arizona, February 28 to March 5, we enjoyed an amazing 23 species of butterflies, including a few of their spring specialties, like Desert Orangetip.

To experience the first spring butterflies, pay close attention to nighttime temperatures. As soon as daytime highs reach into the 50s and 60s and nighttime lows stay above freezing, it is time for butterflies. To learn of probable flight times for some of the single-brooded spring specialties in your area, check any regional guides that cover your area.

Peak Season: Early Summer

Despite the rejuvenation of the insect world and of the butterfly watcher that comes with spring, over much of the country butterfly numbers and diversity remain relatively low until early summer.

For this reason most of the 330 or so NABA 4th of July Butterfly Counts are held in June and July. These counts were started in 1975 and have been held annually since. They were sponsored by the Xerces Society for the first 18 years and then transferred to NABA's sponsorship in 1993. Each count covers a 15-mile-diameter circle and involves a one-day census, by volunteer participants, of all butterflies sighted within that circle. The 4th of July Butterfly Counts emulate National Audubon Society's Christmas Bird Counts (CBCs). Just as few or no CBCs are actually done on Christmas Day, few 4th of July Butterfly

Counts are done on July 4. Most counts are held in the few weeks before and after July 4.

These counts are a wonderful way to monitor butterfly numbers as a barometer of environmental health. Each count is consistently held at relatively the same time each year so that numbers can be compared over time. Most counts attempt to take advantage of the period of peak butterfly diversity and peak numbers of individual butterflies. Some counts fall outside the June and July count period because the time of peak diversity differs for those areas.

In southern New Jersey, the three counts that we have organized and held between mid-June and early July have each recorded between 38 and 50 species in a day. Cumulatively, we have tallied 71 species over the years. In coastal South Carolina, two counts we began in 1993 over the July 4 holiday weekend have now cumulatively tallied 65 species, each recording between 20 and 45 species in a day, depending on that day's weather and the weather that preceded the count. The New Jersey counts, though, have far more observers, skewing the findings; South Carolina would be expected to ultimately show greater diversity.

Arizona and Colorado counts usually see the greatest diversity in the United States. The Gilpin County Count in Colorado recorded 103 species on July 3, 1994, and most other years records more than 80 species. The southeastern Arizona counts are traditionally held in August, later than most other counts, because that is the time of peak diversity. Mexican counts are held following the September rainy season and record the highest diversity of all with a record 169 species tallied on December 31, 1991, on the Puerto Vallarta Count. Check NABA counts for your area to learn when they are held. Chances are a count in your area will be conducted during one of the best times of the year to be afield spotting butterflies.

Peak butterfly diversity often follows the rainy season, a condition that results in lush growth of host plants and wildflowers. While March elfins will nectar on blueberry blossoms and September Gray Hairstreaks find prolific goldenrod, early summer seems to offer the zenith of blooming. Over eons, butterflies have evolved their flight periods to take advantage of these resources. If spring rains never come, all bets are off and butterfly activity can be frighteningly low.

The Dog Days of Summer

Activity in our butterfly garden gets better and better through the summer months, but then it is a pampered backyard garden, mulched and watered when necessary. Such a garden might give a false impression of butterfly abundance at this time of year. In the wild, summer's heat and dryness diminish natural nectar sources, and butterfly numbers and diversity inevitably drop over much of the country, particularly in the South. The intense heat and associated dryness and drought of late July and early August can put a temporary crimp in butterfly watching.

During hot summer days, butterflies frequently are far more active in early morning before the heat develops, and then again in late afternoon as it begins to abate. Species easily seen in early morning may be impossible to find at high noon. We have seen a Question Mark perch in damp shade at midmorning and remain there for the rest of the day.

While the opportunity for big numbers or species counts diminishes as summer progresses, this by no means indicates that there is little for the butterfly watcher to do. For us, summer is a time to explore new areas and look for specialty species like the many uncommon or localized butterflies with brief flight periods and specific habitat and host plant needs. In summer we travel to northern New Jersey bogs in the Highlands, where turtlehead grows, to search for Baltimore Checkerspot, and to the Walkill NWR in search of Silver-bordered Fritillary, and west to grasslands in hopes of Regal Fritillary. In southern New Jersey, the dog days of summer are when we search sandy pine barren road-sides for patches of spotted knapweed and nectaring Dotted Skippers and the striking Leonard's Skipper. We slog through steamy sedge bogs trying to find the localized flashy Dion Skipper and haunt freshwater marsh edges looking for swamp milkweed and nectaring Bronze Coppers. Some summer soon, we plan to venture north for the Northern Metalmark and travel south to the Smoky Mountains in search of the wonderful Diana Fritillary. Summer is for specialties. Know your possibilities and flight periods, and there is always some special butterfly to try for.

While the rest of the country is experiencing the dog days of summer, butterfly watching is at its best in southeastern Arizona because of the monsoon rainy season, which rejuvenates deserts and canyons. Many plants bloom and butterflies rebound. It is a peak time for resident butterflies, and an influx of Mexican species occurs then too. For these reasons Arizona 4th of July Butterfly Counts are traditionally held in early August and have recorded some of the highest diversity in the country. The Ramsey Canyon Count and the Patagonia Count maintain a friendly rivalry: each usually bests 90 species, at times going over 100.

Autumn: Migration

Just as it seems summer will never arrive, during the scorching August heat it seems it will never end. Many resident species drop out of the picture one by one as their flight period ends. Happily, though, other species are migratory, some highly so, and become more numerous as summer draws to a close.

Autumn butterfly migration begins early. Initially it is mostly a trickle, but a trickle that will soon become a stream. Even in early August, while using binoculars to follow a flock of southbound Willet far out over the ocean, we have picked up a Monarch floating south on the northeastern tail winds of a warm August backdoor cold front. By mid-August, northerly winds bring dozens of southbound Monarchs, often seen high over Cape May among the gathering Tree Swallows. Before long, the stream of Monarchs becomes a river, one that will crest in late September and October, the peak of the amazing spectacle of migrating Monarchs. Common Buckeyes, ladies, anglewings, and Mourning Cloaks are migrating too. If you think of spring as flood tide filling the United States and Canada with

Southern species, such as the Clouded Skipper, emigrate north in late summer and fall, spicing up butterfly watching.

butterflies, think of autumn as the ebb, as certain butterflies move south to escape the coming cold.

Yet even as the first Monarchs begin their epic journey south, many other butterflies are venturing north. It is this late summer and fall immigration of southern species that makes this perhaps the most exciting time of year for butterfly watchers. This is when South Carolina spotters look for Zebras and White Peacocks, which come north from Florida. New Mexico watchers look for subtropical strays such as Common Mestra, Boisduval's Yellow, and Crimson Patch. California watchers are on the lookout for Brazilian Skipper and Long-tailed Skipper. In New Jersey, waves of Cloudless Sulphurs pass in late

summer and fall, rarely pausing as they rocket north. It's also when New Jersey spotters may find Long-tailed Skipper, Fiery Skipper, Clouded Skipper, and very rarely Gulf Fritillary — all well north of their normal ranges. Fall is when our own garden hosted its rarest visitor, the huge Brazilian Skipper, on a memorable mid-October day. This skipper, whose nearest regular residence is southern Florida, had emigrated north in the late summer in the pattern of so many one-way migrants.

Fall is when Florida gets strays from Cuba and the Caribbean, true vagrants such as Mimic, Many-banded Daggerwing, and Caribbean Peacock. Nowhere is this vagrant phenomenon better than in south Texas, and butterfly watchers from all over converge on

Late fall produces exciting finds in south Texas, such as the Yellow-tipped Flasher *(above)* and the Guava Skipper *(right)*.

Santa Ana NWR, Bentsen–Rio Grande Valley State Park, and Falcon Dam State Park in October and November to look for the latest arrivals from Mexico. Sometimes these butterflies may come from overflowing healthy broods in tropical areas to the south, sometimes they are refugees from drought conditions and lack of nectar. Nonetheless, every late fall produces exciting finds in south Texas. At Bentsen–Rio Grande Valley State Park a daily list might include 50 species. The list from a week-long trip exploring the lower Rio Grande Valley of Texas may exceed 112 species, including such specialties as Banded Peacock, Blue-eyed Sailor, Mexican Longtail, and Yellow-tipped Flasher.

At this season the Lower Rio Grande Valley of Texas is one of the most productive localities in the United States for butterflying. This is because many of the species that are residents in the valley are essentially tropical

and are rarely if ever found in other areas of the country. Mid-October is the ideal time to visit this area. The weather is comfortable, without the humidity and extreme heat of the summer months. Local butterfly populations have had a chance to build up over the summer, plus many Mexican species are dispersing northward toward the United States border. Blooming purple Joe-pye-weed and asters concentrate butterflies from over a wide area. Goodies can include six or more species of longtail skippers, Sickle-winged Skipper, Mexican Bluewing, Ruby-spotted Swallowtail, Guava Skipper, and Common Mellana. Indeed, Texas in late October is a must for any roving spotter bewitched by butterflies.

Throughout North America late summer and fall is the time of year for rarities — strays and vagrants from more tropical climes — and they add drama and spice to autumnal days afield.

The Last Butterfly of the Season

While the first butterfly of the season is always memorable, somehow we seldom remember the last butterfly of the fall. Normally, our butterfly season in southern New Jersey ends in early to mid-November with the lowering sun and advancing winter temperatures. As crisp nights wilt the last blossoms of fall, we look back and wonder which butterfly was the last. Maybe it was that ragged Red Admiral on the last of the seaside goldenrod, or was it the Common Buckeye we saw migrating around Thanksgiving? One year it was probably that lingering leftover Cloudless Sulphur seen flying down the beach as we watched Northern Gannets diving offshore in December. Another year it was a ragged and determined Monarch flapping purposefully south, heading out over the Delaware Bay on the third of December. A late migrant Osprey seen the same day was significant but overshadowed by the Monarch moving resolutely toward Mexican mountains.

Most years the butterfly season ends with a fizzle as the steady sightings of migrants slow to a trickle, and then one day while watching finches at the feeder you realize the butterflies are gone and have been for a while. While spring begins with a rich promise, the butterflies of late fall seem to evoke only melancholy memories of things past.

One year, with the realization that we couldn't really recall the last butterfly we had seen, either when or where, we attempted to bring closure to our butterfly year by taking one last walk on a warm day at the end of December. It was an unseasonably warm El Niño year, and temperatures had reached over 60°F on the two previous sunny days. We were enticed by Christmas Bird Count reports of butterflies being seen — several Mourning Cloaks, two anglewings, and a mistakenly emerged Orange Sulphur. The heck with chasing the CBC-discovered Golden-crowned Sparrow, we needed a butterfly fix!

It was pushing 68° on warm surging southern air. Nonetheless, the low angle of the winter sun created a challenge for both butterflies and butterfly watchers. In the shade, in the wind, it was decidedly cool. In the sun, however, out of the wind, it was warm . . . warm enough?

We walked the sandy road winding through the pine-oak woods. There were many good signs. A Red Bat was already on the wing, hunting insects, just like us. Spring Peepers called from a pond to the right. Lady Bugs, wasps, and other insects were out — could butterflies be far behind? We covered about a mile before turning around at the dark, sunless cedar swamp. We weren't yet discouraged, but maybe we were being silly to try and extend the season to this degree. Maybe it just wasn't warm enough. After all, it was late December and midwinter.

We spotted the Question Mark flying slowly toward us. It perched briefly, then disappeared as we ran after it. Where? There — perched on a pine trunk in bright sunlight. It may have been worn, a ragged remnant of its former glory, but to us it was lovely, a superb example of the overwintering strategy of the butterfly world. With the warm weather, this individual had emerged from hibernation and would soon reenter its torpor with returning cold weather. We hoped it would make it through the winter and emerge in spring to create yet another generation. We wished it well.

As we walked back to the car, a flock of Cedar Waxwings swept by, and a single Red Crossbill called from high overhead, creating for us an odd juxtaposition of the seasons. The lowering sun brought a chill to the air, and the high, thin clouds heralding the coming rain gave a glow to the late-afternoon sky. The coming strong cold front would seal winter's freeze. This year, at least, we definitively knew when we had seen the last butterfly. As afternoon shadows lengthened, we realized that melancholia and promise could be one, embodied by a small orange butterfly steadfastly awaiting spring.

Winter Doldrums

In most of North America, butterfly activities in winter are but a past memory or a dim hope for the future. Only in southern Florida, southern Texas, southern California, and Mexico can butterflies be found flying through the winter months, and then only if temperatures remain above freezing and it is not too wet.

Winter is a marvelous time to study up on how each butterfly in your area overwinters, either as an egg, a partially grown caterpillar, or as a chrysalis. Just a few species winter as adult butterflies. Some of these early life stages can be searched for during winter months, like the partially grown Red-spotted Purple caterpillar inside its cozy hibernaculum, or swallowtail chrysalids attached to bare branches, the side of a building, or a plant stem left standing in your garden. Such winter quests are for the true specialist, keen observers intent on detecting motionless and often highly camouflaged eggs, caterpillars, and chrysalises.

Another winter pastime is the quest for silkmoth cocoons, which are quite a bit

How to Spot Butterflies

The Promethea Moth's cocoon, a fun winter find, is silked to the host tree and looks like a dangling dead leaf. The adult moth will emerge from it in spring.

bigger and more obvious than butterfly chrysalises. Many of the large silkmoths overwinter as pupae safely protected inside a silken cocoon. The Promethea Moth's cocoon is silked to the host tree and looks like a dead leaf dangling there through the winter. The Cecropia Moth's cocoon stands out, a soft brown swollen area along a twig. Luna Moth cocoons are nearly impossible to find since they fall to the ground when the leaves fall in the autumn.

David Wright shared with us how to use winter as a time to search for the uncommon and unusual Harvester, a species whose larvae are uniquely carnivorous and feed on Woolly Aphids. To find the butterfly one must find the larval host, Woolly Aphids. In winter, David searches for young alder trees, where Woolly Aphids are mostly found, and looks for evidence of aphid damage to the previous year's growth at the ends of limbs. Tunnels through the aphid area made by Harvester larvae are easily seen once you know what to look for. Return the next summer to look for adult Harvesters. Time spent this way in winter is bound to pay off the following season with sightings of this uncommon and localized butterfly. Along the same lines, winter is an excellent time to explore and look for specialized habitats. Bogs and meadows discovered on winter walks have rewarded us with butterflies the following season.

If these suggestions for distracting you from the cold-weather doldrums do not strike your fancy, you'll just have to travel to our southern border or even farther if you wish to see winter butterflies.

Around the Country

W E WERE ON A REGULARLY scheduled flight, but our eager group and gear filled the plane and barely left room for the mail sacks and cargo bound for Arctic Village. On the flight north from Fairbanks, broken clouds dappled the tundra and created fleeting patterns and illusions far below.

Butterfly watching near Arctic Village *(right)*, 125 miles north of the Arctic Circle, was an adventure full of new finds such as this Silvery Blue *(above)*.

It was an eventful flight, routine yet spectacular for we easterners getting our first look at Alaska. Beyond the lustrous Yukon River, the clouds were lower and forced the pilot to decrease altitude. We saw our first Dall Sheep, white against gray granite, out the aircraft window, just a few hundred yards off the wing tip, or so it seemed as the pilot picked his way north, around mountains, down valleys, and through passes to avoid the heavy clouds above. We easily picked out Tundra Swans on ponds below. As the Cessna banked tightly to line up for final approach on the gravel airstrip, we felt some relief. Our first bush-flying experience, an everyday routine for those dwelling in the Far North, had left us sheepishly nervous.

As we unloaded the plane at Arctic Village there was already an exciting sense of adventure — the terminal was a 20' × 20' open-air wooden building, with a Say's Phoebe coming and going as she built her nest on the rafters inside. It was late June and we were about 125 miles north of the Arctic Circle, in the foothills of the south slope of the Brooks Range. This town

How to Spot Butterflies

of about 200 residents was our jump-off point for a float trip in the Arctic National Wildlife Refuge, 19 million acres of wilderness in northeastern Alaska. We were on a busman's holiday — a tour planned with eight friends and fellow naturalists, booked with Wilderness Birding Adventures out of Anchorage. We eagerly anticipated Arctic birds, bears — and butterflies.

We had a five-hour layover in Arctic Village before the bush plane would carry us and our gear, in five shuttle flights, over the Brooks Range to the Canning River to begin our float trip — 11 days and 60 miles — to the Arctic Ocean. With five hours to kill we began our Arctic birding and butterflying. "Let's get started," Sheri Williamson, co-director of the Southeastern Arizona Bird Observatory, said simply. "No problem," was Linda Dunne's eager reply.

There was a lovely tundra lake just beyond the airstrip, where we soon found both Common and Pacific Loons, Lesser Yellowlegs calling from stunted spruces around the edge,

Arctic Terns flying over, and our first jaeger. After about an hour the sky opened and the sun broke through. Temperatures soon rose to over 70°F.

The tundra habitat along the lakeshore came alive with insects: flies, bumblebees, midges, moths, mosquitoes. Butterflies weren't abundant, but they were easily found as we worked the vegetation and walked about. Arctic butterflies are generally cryptically patterned — camouflage that helps them survive lengthy periods of cold and inactivity dictated by the changeable Arctic weather. Many are dark — the better to absorb heat quickly when sunlight is available. Because of this, we flushed most before we saw them, yet were fairly successful in following them with binoculars and finding where they landed. Then we crept up for good looks and photos, ever mindful not to crush the abundant Arctic wildflowers: mountain avens, Labrador lousewort, moss campion, bog rosemary, Lap-

This Arctic Grayling blends exceptionally well with its tundra habitat.

land rosebay, and so many more. With a slow approach, butterflies allowed us to get within inches.

Life butterflies came fast. "I've got an alpine here," called Linda. "I'm not sure which one, maybe a Banded Alpine." "Hold on," Sheri yelled back, "I'm working on a fritillary — I think it's a Mountain Fritillary, I'm not positive." "I've got an Arctic over here," called her husband, Tom Wood (also a co-director of SABO). "It looks like a Jutta Arctic."

Like kids in a candy store, we rushed from one butterfly to the next. Identification was tough. Because of the bush flight's weight limitation, we didn't have our usual battery of butterfly books and guides. We hastily compared each new butterfly to the plates from James Scott's treatise, *The Butterflies of North America*, blasphemously cut out of the three-pound book and stapled together back home in a weight-saving measure.

Our hosts and guides, Bob Dittrick and Lisa Moorehead, soon joined us. Their knowledge of Arctic ecology and tundra wildflowers added immeasurably to the experience. "There, on the cranberry flowers, a Cranberry Blue." "Over by the patch of moss campion — a Banded Alpine." "Here's another, this is different — an Arctic Grayling!" With each exclamation we all converged for good looks and photos, kneeling in a circle around the butterfly, intently watching, taking photographs, looking for all the world like a herd of Musk-ox on the tundra, except we were facing in, not out! An Athabaskan boy on an ATV watched from the airport road. Though this was an outpost, they had seen plenty of birders at Arctic Village, but butter-

The black coloration near the body helps this fritillary absorb the sun's warmth.

fliers were something new! Our personal favorite was a cooperative Grizzled Skipper, not only our first ever, but one we had longed for in the East, a widespread but uncommon mountain species once found in northern New Jersey, yet now extirpated, vanished from much of the East.

It was butterflying far different from any we had done before. The arctics and alpines, when flushed, would fly off strongly, then pitch down into the ground, hugging tundra vegetation. When we refound them, they appeared half-buried in the thick lichens, fantastically camouflaged. They were lateral baskers, perching close-winged, but clearly orienting toward the sun — laying over so that the wing surface faced the sun and absorbed as much warmth as possible from it. Nowhere have we been more aware that butterflies are solar-powered than during this Arctic adventure.

The Arctic weather is highly changeable. Low clouds, fog, or wind off the Arctic Ocean can lower late June temperatures to 40°F with no insect activity. But if the sun breaks through, 20 minutes later temperatures can rise to 65°F or better and butterflies will be everywhere. Clouds crossing the sun again can end butterfly activity as quickly as it started. While birds can be watched anytime in the land of the midnight sun, we quickly learned to butterfly hard when the opportunity presented itself. One windless, clear and warm evening we watched butterflies until ten o'clock at night.

The drone of the inbound bush plane ended our reverie. It was time to return to the airstrip and load up — rafts, tents, and gear for the five flights needed to get us all to the Canning River. Many adventures awaited, from watching a Gyrfalcon aerie on a riverside cliff to the awe of Caribou herds on the coastal

A Grizzled Skipper's covering of bristly "hairs" insulates against heat loss.

plain, to mystical encounters with elusive Arctic butterflies. As we packed up, we all agreed that this had been the best airport layover any of us had ever had, with its infusion of tundra butterflies, the sparkling wings of the high Arctic summer. In the next 11 days we would identify 16 species of butterflies and photograph a number of others to be identified later, all new to us — all Arctic specialties.

The Far North

Even among experienced naturalists, few would guess at the abundance of butterflies in the Arctic. Despite our reading and planning, we were unprepared for the quality of butterfly watching there. While Arctic species diversity is lower than that of warmer areas to the south, butterflies are numerous and a major player in the Arctic tundra ecosystem. Surprisingly, 51 species of six families are known from the New World Arctic north of treeline. Many species have a two-year life cycle — they are biennial, flying only every other year. This is because the caterpillar takes two years to mature because of the extremely brief one- to two-month Arctic summer. If this seems unusual, consider that the Woolly Bear moth caterpillar in the Arctic may live as a caterpillar for 13 years or more before pupating and emerging as an adult.

A number of strategies allow Arctic butterflies to live in the Far North. With only one or two months warm enough for caterpillar growth, mid-June to mid-August at the most, many species remain in the caterpillar stage for prolonged periods, sometimes several years. When the brief summer finally comes to the Arctic, plants grow rapidly, wildflowers abound, and nectar is readily available to adult butterflies; the 24 hours of daylight during the Arctic summer allows butterflies to be active for lengthy periods, sometimes until 10:00 P.M. or later. The cryptic coloration of many Arctic butterflies may assist mainly during long periods of cold-induced inactivity when they are forced to hide deep in tundra vegetation. Basking is frequent, though, when the sun is available, and many Arctic butterflies are black or have black markings near the body to help them readily absorb the sun's radiant energy and warm up. In addition, Arctic species are covered with dense, bristly "hairs" which help insulate them against heat loss. Although Arctic butterfly diversity is low, there are usually many individuals of a given species.

Arctic and alpine butterfly species are a treat for the butterfly enthusiast and are readily available in many areas of Alaska and

Canada. Each issue of NABA's quarterly journal, *American Butterflies*, includes a "definitive destination" article written by knowledgeable butterfly spotters that chronicles a site, includes detailed directions, and lists species to be found and their status. Peter Taylor and Paul Klassen's NABA article about butterflying in Manitoba invites butterfliers to visit between late May and early August, with early July being the time of peak diversity. Their article showcases 18 different areas that are accessible, including boreal forest, the tundra at Churchill, and a number of short-grass and tall-grass prairie areas. Churchill is a well-known birding location, but butterflying can be excellent there as well, with 45 species recorded, including Theano Alpine, Ross' Alpine, White-veined Arctic, Melissa Arctic, Polixenes Arctic, Polaris Fritillary, Labrador Sulphur, and Hecla Sulphur. If you are a birder, though, be advised that the best butterflying at Churchill occurs later than the peak birding time. Birders arrive for "ice-out," during the first week of June, and butterfly watchers need to visit later, between late June and early August.

Alpine and Arctic-Alpine Zone butterflying is easily possible in many of the western mountains of southern Canada and the northern United States. The roads and trails through Banff and Jasper National Parks in Alberta, Canada, offer excellent access to a variety of high-altitude habitats. Andrew Warren's definitive destination NABA article details Apex Park in the Front Range of Colorado as a great place for Milbert's Tortoiseshell and Northern Checkerspot and such high-altitude specialties as Large Marble and Phoebus Parnassian. Gilpin County, Colorado, in the Rockies west of Denver, gener-

The Arctic summer's 24 hours of daylight allows butterflies to be active for lengthy periods. Sheri Williamson watches a butterfly close at hand at 10 o'clock at night.

This immaculate Milbert's Tortoiseshell was found in Colorado's Front Range.

ally has one of, if not *the* highest, NABA 4th of July Butterfly Counts in all of North America — 103 species were recorded on the count there in 1994! This count combines alpine meadows, forest, and grazing lands, habitat diversity that creates a mecca for butterfliers. Numerous high-altitude species can be relatively easy to find there. Jim Mori and Ray Coyle's definitive destination article about the Sonora Pass through the Sierra Nevadas in eastern California entices with details about access to unusual habitats such as high-altitude wet meadows and barren rock knolls and accounts of 90 species in the area, including

Chryxus Arctic, Ridings' Satyr, Johnson's Hairstreak, Sooty Hairstreak, seven species of fritillaries, Lustrous Copper, Ruddy Copper, and Northern Checkerspot. Robert Pyle's article in *American Butterflies* about the Magdalena Alpine directs readers to accessible arctic-alpine, high-altitude rockslide areas in northern New Mexico, Utah, Colorado, Wyoming, and southern Montana — areas that are also home to Melissa Arctic, Lustrous Copper, and Rockslide Checkerspot. If Alaskan or Canadian High Arctic butterflying is not easily accessible, as it isn't for most of us, try high-altitude alpine tundra habitat butterfly watching, readily available and immensely satisfying in our western mountain parks.

The West

We were visiting Garden Canyon in the Huachuca Mountains, near Sierra Vista, Arizona. The Huachucas are one of the many mountain ranges or "sky islands" that rise from the surrounding grasslands. Rising to over 7,000 feet, the increased altitude, cool temperatures, and moisture allow for healthy coniferous forests near the peaks.

The occasion was the second Biennial NABA Members' Meeting, held in August to coincide with expected peak diversity. More than 200 butterfly enthusiasts had converged on Sierra Vista, many for our first visit to study and enjoy the area's remarkable butterfly fauna. We broke into small groups for field trips. Our leader was Jim Brock, Arizona butterfly legend and coauthor with Richard Bailowitz of *Butterflies of Southeastern Arizona* and author of the *Checklist of Butterflies and Skippers of Southeastern Arizona*.

We began our hike near the mouth of Garden Canyon, around 5,000 feet in elevation. Our plan was to hike to Sawmill Spring near the summit, at about 7,000 feet. We planned to ascend from scrubby grassland habitat up into a lush Ponderosa Pine forest. What makes butterflying so excellent here is the habitat change as one goes higher — a four-mile trail passes through several life zones. As the vegetation changes with elevation, so do the butterflies. Also, the year-round presence of water — springs, seeps, and a stream — and

the attendant quantity and variety of wildflowers, creates year-round nectar sources and puddling opportunities. More than 135 species of butterflies have been recorded in Garden Canyon — around half of the total for all of southeastern Arizona.

The excitement began right in the parking area near the picnic grounds. The rainy season had begun late, but recent cloudbursts had left numerous puddles in the gravel road. At one, Reakirt's Blues, Ceraunus Blues, and Marine Blues puddled by the dozens. Cloudless Sulphurs dashed about and we spotted numerous Sleepy Oranges and one Mexican Yellow. Skippers were abundant, but large, dramatic, and cooperative Dull Firetips stood out as they nectared at Mexican star thistle. A surprise, even for our veteran leader, was the number of Moon-marked Skippers, aptly named and easily watched. Jim explained that it was a great year for them, the best he'd seen,

The Moon-marked Skipper is a specialty of southwestern canyons.

Nabokov's Satyr, named for one of the first and most famous butterfly watchers.

and we recorded about 60 that day, all in the lower reaches of the canyon.

About halfway up the canyon, we hit paydirt: stands of blooming *Baccharis* had attracted a plethora of butterflies. Metalmarks! Three species were quickly separated: an Arizona, many Zelas, and an Ares Metalmark.

Heading higher still, we entered the true pine forest. Here trailside seeps attracted California Sisters — spectacular above and be-low. Variegated Fritillaries were abundant, yet we tried in vain to separate out a Mexican Fritillary . . . perhaps we were between broods. Two-tailed Swallowtails were abundant, large, and spectacular, some nectaring, some puddling. Personal favorites were the numerous checkerspots: Theona, Tiny, and Black. Jim told us that the Black Checkerspot was the pride of Garden Canyon: its range in the United States is totally limited to southeastern Arizona, where the caterpillar feeds on Indian paintbrush. Despite his years of experience, Jim Brock is far from jaded. We went on to tally eight Black Checkerspots, and he beamed with pride.

Nearing Sawmill Trail, we were forced to turn around, lest we be late for the afternoon conference lectures and workshops. Hurrying down the canyon we paused to catch our breath and recheck a lush *Baccharis* thicket. The expected Leda Ministreaks and a Juniper Hairstreak greeted us, but the tame Great Purple Hairstreak, a glowing jewel, was a first for all of us. It was a species that had eluded us in the East. We knew mistletoe, its host plant, had to be somewhere nearby.

Nearing the picnic area, one more wonder appeared. Here we found a Nabokov's Satyr, an early member of the second brood, an immaculate individual of this evocative species — named for one of the first and most famous true butterfly watchers, writer Vladimir Nabokov. Satyrs are always special — so subtle, often secretive, always ephemeral, yet an enduring memory.

Butterfly activity had slowed partly from the midday heat, but more certainly from the loss of the sun. Heavy clouds were now building overhead, presaging expected afternoon rain, the normal pattern for August in the sky islands of Arizona. We had tallied about 38 species, a good number for butterflies anywhere, yet only average for Garden Canyon. Fifty species is not unexpected there in a day. Garden Canyon is one of the many spectacular natural areas in southeastern Arizona. The various canyons are a must for the butterfly watcher, offering a myriad of winged wonders in season and some sightings at almost any time of the year. You will never regret your visit. For us, southeastern Arizona in August remains one of our absolute favorite butterfly spots — a place to which we return often in our minds and as often as we can in person.

Southeastern Arizona has long been nirvana for butterfly enthusiasts. The sheer abundance of species is amazing, with more than 240 species recorded there — about a third of all the species recorded in North America north of Mexico, including many found nowhere else in the United States. Two factors account for such remarkable diversity. First is the proximity to Mexico and the well-known phenomenon of southern species straying north across the border during the late-summer and fall monsoon season. The second factor is that southeastern Arizona contains a rich diversity of habitat and associated flora and fauna, from low desert to high desert and grasslands to Canadian Zone coniferous forests. In the Santa Catalinas, north of Tucson, the Catalina Highway ascends almost 7,000 feet from arid mesquite washes to the top of Mount Lemmon where ski resorts are found. Biologically, this is akin to driving from south Florida scrub to the White Mountains in New Hampshire! It is no mystery, therefore, why the butterfly variety is so great.

Good butterfly areas in this region include some of the classic birding canyons: Madera and Box Canyons in the Santa Rita Mountains; Cave Creek Canyon in the Chiricahuas; and Ramsey, Garden, and Carr Canyons in the Huachucas. Good butterfly canyons require many of the same attributes as birding canyons: water, for the benefit of butterflies and their nectar sources, and access — a road ascending the canyon through the various altitudinal life zones.

The southeastern Arizona lowlands should be explored as well. We've enjoyed excellent butterfly spotting at The Nature Conservancy's Patagonia-Sonoita Creek Preserve and in the San Pedro Riparian National Conservation Area — species such as Leda Ministreak, Acmon Blue, Ceraunus Blue, Marine Blue, Western Pygmy-Blue, Palmer's Metalmark, Fatal Metalmark, Bordered Patch, Tiny Checkerspot, Queen, Viceroy, and Golden-headed Scallopwing to name a few. Stands of *Senecio* were the key to finding butterflies during one early March visit, and similarly blooming *Baccharis* and puddles attracted butterflies during an August visit. Sheri Williamson and Tom Wood have taken us to other little-known butterfly hotspots, such as Gold Gulch in Bisbee, where we saw hundreds of puddling Reakirt's, Ceraunus, and Marine Blues, more than a dozen Mormon Metalmarks, and our first Common Streaky-Skippers. At Slaughter Ranch, an oasis in the San Bernardino Valley, on an early March day Acmon Blues nectared on wildflowers in the lawn while we watched our first Desert Or-

Despite temperatures over 100°F, blooming *Baccharis* along Aravaipa Creek attracted Fatal Metalmarks and many other butterflies.

angetip dash by and disappear across the arid lands beyond. We'll never forget our first visit to Arizona when we journeyed to Aravaipa Canyon in August. The temperature was well over 100°F and the only shade was in our vehicle. Along the gravel road, fallen fruit from a pomegranate tree had drawn in an Empress Leilia, our first. Beside Aravaipa Creek stands of blooming *Baccharis* held Fatal Metalmarks, Queens, Ceraunus Blues, and a Palmer's Metalmark, and the unbearable heat was quickly forgotten. Regardless of the elevation, southeastern Arizona offers some of the most satisfying butterfly spotting in the country.

Farther east, the Rio Grande Valley of south Texas is also excellent for butterflies. Well-known birding spots such as Sabal Palm Grove Sanctuary, Bentsen–Rio Grande Valley State Park, Santa Ana NWR, and Falcon Dam are all stellar for butterfly spotting as well. Extensive trails through diverse natural habitats make this area one of the top butterfly-watching spots in the country. October and November are judged best in the Lower Rio Grande Valley, when more than 50 species are possible in a day. Winter is slowest, when cooler temperatures prevail. White-striped Longtail, Banded Peacock, and Coyote Skipper can be found among the 200-plus species known from the area. Some of our favorites from the area are Goodson's Greenstreak, Dusky-blue Groundstreak, Red-bordered Metalmark, Mexican Bluewing, and Common Mestra.

Good butterfly watching in the Southwest is certainly not limited to Arizona and Texas. NABA's definitive destination articles in *American Butterflies* offer some of the most detailed accounts of western butterfly hotspots. Our visit to Texas was helped greatly by Mike

How to Spot Butterflies

Rickard's NABA article on Bentsen–Rio Grande State Park, just as Jim Brock's article on Garden Canyon in the Huachuca Mountains helped prepare us for a trip to Arizona. Stephen Cary's article on Sitting Bull Falls in the Guadalupe Mountains of New Mexico lures us with such goodies as Chinati Checkerspot, Dotted Checkerspot, Sandia Hairstreak, and Morrison's Skipper. Jack Levy's article on Anza-Borrego Desert State Park in southern California, near the Mexican border, entices us to low desert where Sonoran Blue, Gray Marble, Becker's White, Sara Orangetip, and California Giant Skipper all might be found.

Just as butterflies have special adaptations for life in high-altitude areas, they have special ways to conform to life in the sometimes intense heat and sun of the Southwest. To beat the heat, butterflies are most active in the relative cool of early morning and late afternoon — and far less active in the heat of midday. In contrast to the temperate zone, where butterflies are active in bright sun and inactive when clouds pass over, in Texas we have seen butterflies absent in intense sun and heat, but reappear and become more active when clouds cover the sun. In hot climates, butterflies often estivate during the day, becoming inactive. We have watched a Moon-marked Skipper crawl under a ledge, out of the sun in a cool, shady crevice of rock and remain there for hours at midday. In the heat of midday, shady areas may be the most productive. Remember, in the heat of the Southwest, the best butterflying is early and diminishes greatly by noontime: butterflies take siestas too in the hot and arid Southwest. Also remember that in the rainy season, butterflying is best in the morning, since showers usually come by early afternoon.

Goodson's Greenstreak, a tropical hairstreak, strays north to south Texas.

The Eastern Forest

We have explored butterfly opportunities at both ends of North America, the Arctic, and the tropics, but there are many outstanding places in between. The eastern mixed forests, with associated bogs, meadows, and fields, offer consistent, if seasonal, butterfly adventure.

Butterfly hotspots are areas that combine, to varying degrees, ease of access with good diversity and/or unusual finds. Whenever we travel, no matter what the reason, we try to be prepared for the butterflies of the area. Ahead of time we study maps that may show public lands and topographic maps that show habitats. We peruse bird-finding guides or butterfly-finding guides, if they exist for the area, to learn of potential hotspots. Combining the books and the maps, we set up a route that will take us through different habitats and natural areas accessible by road or trail.

In just this way years ago we discovered the vast Francis Marion National Forest in coastal South Carolina. A network of little-traveled roads through the forest has provided us with some of our best summer butterflying. We've learned to be on the lookout for good nectar plants such as pickerelweed, buttonbush, lippia, sweet white clover, rattlesnake master, sweet pepperbush, *Pluchea*, and narrow-leaved vervain; butterflies follow. We've learned to search for essential host plants such as switch cane and been fortunate to find Reversed Roadside-Skipper and Creole Pearly-Eye. Passion-vine often produces Gulf Fritillaries, and sugarberry trees draw in Hackberry Emperors and American Snouts. To comple-

Searching for butterflies in Francis Marion National Forest, South Carolina.

ment the forest's many habitats we've also explored other public natural areas such as Moore's Landing, Hampton Plantation State Park, Santee Coastal Reserve, Santee Delta Wildlife Management Area, Samworth Game Management Area, and Huntington Beach State Park.

One return trip from South Carolina we detoured to explore the Great Dismal Swamp near Norfolk, Virginia, using the NABA definitive destination article written by Jeffrey Glassberg as our guide. Great Purple Hairstreak, Southern and Creole Pearly-Eyes, and Duke's Skipper eluded us, but we did enjoy a puddle party of four species of swallowtails and close encounters with several dozen Zebra Swallowtails. We'll never be able to drive through this great area again without considering a butterfly detour.

Known butterfly hotspots in the eastern forests include other NABA definitive destinations such as Ocala National Forest in northern Florida. Marc Minno's write-up highlights unique habitats and species such as Ocola Skipper, Cofaqui Giant-Skipper, Lace-winged Roadside-Skipper, Dusky Roadside-Skipper, Dotted Skipper, Arogos Skipper, Little Yellow, Pipevine Swallowtail, Zebra Swallowtail, Great Purple Hairstreak, and Goatweed Leafwing. Charles Covell's write-up about Pisgah National Forest and Harmon Den Wildlife Refuge in North Carolina lures us with tales of such specialties as Diana Fritillary, Green Comma, and Pipevine Swallowtail. Rick Cech's piece on the Appalachian Mountains of West Virginia and Virginia shares information about where to go in Fork Creek Wildlife Management

How to Spot Butterflies

Look for native grasslands and protected prairie habitats when butterfly watching in the Midwest and West and you will be rewarded.

Area, Larenim State Park, and Brattons Run Shale Barrens in George Washington National Forest for Gemmed Satyr, Grizzled Skipper, Harvester, and Olympia Marble. Moving north, Jeffrey Glassberg's definitive destination article about Ward Pound Ridge Reservation in Westchester County, New York, just north of New York City, beckons us with species such as Silvery Checkerspot, Harris' Checkerspot, Zabulon Skipper, Mulberry Wing, and Black Dash. A New England definitive destination written by Brian Cassie directs readers to the northeastern border of New Hampshire with Maine for such species as Canadian Tiger Swallowtail, Silvery Blue, Bog Fritillary, Green Comma, Hoary Comma, and the dapper Arctic Skipper.

These are just a few of the many, many butterfly-spotting areas of the vast eastern forests that have been detailed in *American Butterflies* to date. There are many others. Use the butterfly-finding techniques outlined earlier: first find protected public lands, then seek out meadows, fields, bogs, abandoned railroad right-of-ways, and power-line or utility right-of-ways. Use range maps and flight-period information to determine what you might see on your visit. Then all you need is a sunny day!

Midwestern Prairies

For a different butterfly experience, try the wide-open spaces of rolling hills and sprawling grasslands of our country's heartland. Midwestern prairies are excellent but-

Gray Copper is a midwestern prairie specialty.

terfly-finding areas. Regal Fritillary may be endangered in the East, and even rare and local in Wisconsin, but farther west, in Minnesota, Missouri, and Nebraska, they can still be enjoyed in numbers. These magnificent butterflies have a protracted flight period. In an average year, Regal Fritillaries fly from early July to the end of August. To see prairie butterflies such as Regal Fritillaries, Dakota Skipper, and Ottoe Skipper, Ann Swengel's NABA articles direct people to Buffalo River State Park, Pipestone National Monument, and Bicentennial Prairie in Minnesota; Prairie State Park in Missouri; Rowe Sanctuary along the Platte River Valley in central Nebraska; and Nelson Dewey State Park in Wisconsin. Look for native grasslands and protected prairie habitats when butterfly watching in the Midwest and you will be rewarded.

John Shuey's NABA definitive destination article about Indiana Dunes National Lakeshore and Hoosier Prairie State Nature Preserve in northwestern Indiana directs readers to a variety of habitats, including lakeshore dunes, oak barrens, fens, sedge meadows, and remnant prairie. Here Gray Copper, Byssus Skipper, and Ottoe Skipper are found in season, and you can readily watch migrating Monarchs in fall. We have enjoyed Monarch migration at the Concordia hawkwatch, north of Milwaukee, on the shore of Lake Michigan. Lakeshores can clearly act as leading lines for butterfly migration much as they function to concentrate migratory birds. We have enjoyed early fall butterflies in famous bird haunts near Duluth in Minnesota and at Crex Meadows WMA in northwestern Wisconsin.

Prairies are a precious and shrinking natural habitat with some butterflies completely dependent on them. The mixture of native grasses and wildflowers that makes a prairie a prairie has largely been lost to intensive farming and grazing. Holding onto remnant prairies today involves maintenance strategies such as prescribed burns. Ann Swengel, who has extensively studied prairies and prairie butterflies, feels that while these fires may stimulate the native grasses and wildflowers and curb other species, they are very harmful to insects. The insects are killed in the fires and must repopulate prairie preserves from nearby areas not yet burned. Ann believes that low-intensity grazing and cutting might better mimic the days when herds of grazing Bison, Pronghorn, and other herbivores maintained the prairies naturally. Managing the few remaining prairie preserves is tricky business if butterflies are to be considered too.

Urban Butterflying

No matter where you live, or where you travel, butterflies are never far away. Only in the rain- and fog-shrouded Pacific Northwest rain forest region can butterflies be truly difficult to find. We once spent a week in fog-bound and rain-soaked coastal Alaska at Cordova on Prince William Sound and saw a total of five individual butterflies, all Mustard Whites! As you may guess, we also never saw the sun. The same sort of wet, overcast weather diminished a brief trip to coastal California one spring.

Butterflies are everywhere, but you have to convince yourself that they are there to be found — even in adverse conditions or in urban areas. Proof that butterflies can be found anywhere: more than 120 species have been found within 50 miles of the center of New York City, accessible to more than 15 million people. Butterflies are found right in the city, and daily lists of more than 20 species can be recorded at places such as Pelham Bay Park, Van Cortlandt Park, or Jamaica Bay NWR, where more than 70 species have been recorded over time, including one unusual vagrant, a Small Tortoiseshell from Europe. On the West Coast, more than 70 species can be found in coastal Los Angeles County, despite its urban character, by exploring places such as South Coast Botanical Gardens, Santa Monica Mountains National Recreation Area, and Angeles National Forest. Similarly, John Hafernik and Harriet Reinhard shared a definitive destination article about San Francisco's urban jungle and the 26 species found there by exploring Twin Peaks near Glen Canyon Park, Bay View Hill just north of Candlestick Park, Baker Beach and Lobos Creek, and San Bruno Mountain State and County Parks.

True, in many parts of the country, little information is yet available on butterfly finding, but one of the most exciting aspects of butterfly spotting is the very fact that in many regions it is still in its infancy. We have shared with you one of the best sources of butterfly-watching hotspots, the North American Butterfly Association's journal, *American Butterflies*. Over time NABA's journal will feature dozens of other sites. New regional books on butterflies are being published at a rapid rate. These offer excellent local information. If your area is not yet covered with such detailed information, go out and find butterflies on your own. Keep good records and perhaps you may find yourself writing about a discovered site in one of NABA's definitive destination articles. Armed with binoculars, a good field guide, and a knowledge of butterfly-finding techniques, you can make major discoveries in your area, discoveries that can aid in our growing knowledge of butterfly status and distribution. Over time, such new knowledge can only lead to wider and stronger butterfly conservation. Have fun, good luck, and enjoy the unexpected wonders of butterfly watching.

Gardening for Butterflies

E ACH YEAR OUR GARDEN creeps into the yard a bit more and the mowed portion diminishes, much to our delight and the delight of butterflies, moths, a host of other insects, and hummingbirds and many other birds. Our passion for butterfly gardening began years ago with a small pot of bee balm, hurriedly uprooted and

Plant a butterfly garden and they will come! Be sure to offer nectar from spring through fall. Asters (*above,* with Orange Sulphur) and verbena (*right,* with Red Admiral) are especially good in fall.

passed on by a friend. The array of nectaring visitors that first summer so amazed us that we've been avid butterfly and hummingbird gardeners ever since. Indeed, plant a butterfly garden and they will come! Certainly there is nothing quite like discovering a wild area full of butterflies, but enticing an endless parade of butterflies to your own garden where you can study them at leisure during a lunch break, on days off, and any time you step out the back door is going to accelerate your learning curve, offer incredible photographic opportunities, and soothe the spirit as you simply sit back and enjoy.

In recent years gardening for butterflies has caught the imagination of many — thankfully, for butterflies! Each successful butterfly garden is likely to attract the attention of other gardeners who have grown weary of the same old beds of geraniums, impatiens, marigolds, petunias, or whatever the norm is in your area. Many gardeners are ready to be daring and try something new that brings so much additional pleasure in the form of flying jewels — butterflies and hummingbirds. It is a growing trend. Schoolyard habitats, including butter-

fly gardens, are sprouting and flourishing throughout the country. Volunteer efforts by scout groups and garden and nature clubs are responsible for butterfly gardens on town properties, and most nature centers take pride in having one or several butterfly gardens.

Beware of instant butterfly gardens and butterfly meadows out of a can. Many learn the hard way that such a garden might pro-

Schoolyard gardens and meadows can be terrific outdoor classrooms.

duce a lot of flash and color the first year, but it soon fizzles out to a very disappointing and unproductive space in the yard. There is a bit more to butterfly gardening than pouring seeds out of a can, but with a bit of reading, thought, and planning you will be amazed at how selective efforts produce a garden that is attractive to butterflies the very first year and that will get better and better with each year. Another misconception is that bigger plants

are better and create a garden faster. Actually, you are better off purchasing young perennials than older rootbound plants. The roots of young plants adapt more quickly and in one season will grow to be just as large as the huge plant you initially thought you needed to purchase.

Before heading off to your local nursery, first put considerable thought into a butterfly habitat plan. The first and most important task is choosing a sunny location for your garden. Remember that butterflies are solar-powered; they need to be warm and dry to fly. Choose the sunniest part of your yard for the garden, or plant a series of gardens to take advantage of sunny spots as the sun moves across your yard. Butterflies will move from garden to garden with the sun. Do not cut down your woods to create a sunny spot. Use some of your lawn area instead.

Since butterflies are delicate and can be blown about easily, your garden design needs sheltered areas. Gardens on edges, up against shrubby or forested areas or a fence, can offer considerable protection from strong winds. Gardens placed out in very open areas take advantage of sun all day long, but will be more attractive if they also offer shelter. A horseshoe-shaped garden of flowering shrubs offers nectar out of the wind on at least one side no matter which direction the wind is blowing, even on the windiest day. Butterflies can also overheat. At such times they slip into areas of shade or dappled sunlight and become sedentary. So be sure to provide such areas within your butterfly habitat.

Diversity, a key factor, should be the next consideration in your plan. A wide-open lawn with a lone butterfly garden in the middle of it will attract some activity, but probably very little compared to an area with lots of options. Incorporate into your plan formal and informal gardens, natural or weedy areas or edges, plantings of native trees and shrubs, a wildflower meadow if room permits, and the minimal amount of lawn you need. With such a plan butterfly activity is bound to soar.

Draft a garden plan for your property considering sun, shelter, diversity, and utilizing what already exists. Learn which butterflies occur in your area and research their host plants. You'll probably find that many of the native trees, shrubs, vines, and weedy plants that may already exist in your yard are important larval foodplants. For instance, the Eastern Tiger Swallowtails we enjoy each summer lay their eggs on a tuliptree we planted as a shade tree. 'Olive' Juniper Hairstreaks occur in our garden because of redcedars we planted as a natural privacy hedge.

Think of your plan as a work in progress. It will no doubt evolve as you learn more and as you get new ideas by visiting other gardens. The plan can be carried out in stages; you could tackle a different garden each year — meadow, pond area, shrub border, whatever — but you'll find it very helpful to work from a rough long-term plan. If a permanent irrigation or watering system is possible, consider it early on, before you've planted hundreds of dollars' worth of plants that you will not want to dig up to put in water lines. In a long-term plan, try to envision what you would like the garden to look like ten years down the line,

or even twenty. Remember, too, some plants grow tall! Place them in the back of your design.

Once you've drawn up a plan and know where you want your garden, choose the plants. This step is not as simple as you may think. We are fortunate today to have so much information available on butterfly gardening, though for the beginner there is almost too much information on the subject; some butterfly gardening books take a broad-brush approach and try to address the entire country, an impossible task. There are dramatic regional differences in the butterflies to be found, larval foodplants they need, plants that will succeed, and how attractive certain plants will be to local butterflies. These differences are often noted state by neighboring state, county by neighboring county, and often even neighborhood by nearby neighborhood.

This being the case, you can learn a great deal by visiting a variety of butterfly gardens in your area for plant selection ideas, as well as layout and design ideas. Butterfly gardeners are nearly always delighted to share their labor of love with new wildlife gardeners. You'll find that one gardener knows another, makes the overture call on your behalf, and, before you know it, the next month of weekends is lined up with garden visits. Visit arboretums and public gardens in your state and nearby states to learn firsthand what may work in your area. Since each garden is different, visit all that are within a reasonable drive. Another not-so-surprising source of information is local nurseries; visit them to see which plants are adorned with nectaring wild butterflies.

As much as possible, you'll need to visit all

of these learning sites through the seasons to master the art of offering nectar to each season's company of butterflies. If you are weak in early bloomers, visit local gardens and nurseries in spring. The same is true to learn of plants that flower through the heat of summer. A garden with no nectar in fall is indeed sad as the final waves of Monarchs continue to parade through. Ask fellow gardeners which of their plants flower past the first frost. Each garden has a history of tried and failed plants. You can benefit greatly by learning from these gardeners and save yourself the growth pains they have already gone through.

Butterfly houses, or living butterfly exhibits, have long been popular in England, where there are more than 60. In 1988 the first butterfly house opened in the United States; in ten years' time there are more than 20. Our favorites are those with an outdoor learning component, such as Butterfly World at Tradewinds Park in Florida and the Day Butterfly Center at Calloway Gardens in Georgia. They both have outdoor gardens planted with nectar and host plants that attract countless wild butterflies. Of course we are dazzled each time we visit the indoor live exhibits of exotic butterflies and appreciate the terrific photographic opportunities, but the outdoor setting draws us out each time we visit. Hours go by as we explore Butterfly World's arbors, draped with host plants such as passion-vine, and look for caterpillars, chrysalises, and egg-laying adults. One other favorite living butterfly exhibit, though on a much smaller scale, is Butterfly Barn in McClellanville, South Carolina, probably because it specializes in native species rather than exotic species like so many

Butterfly houses or living exhibits are growing in popularity (Cockrell Center).

other butterfly houses. It also has an outdoor component and a nursery with butterfly nectar plants for sale.

Many mail-order nurseries now include information on plants that are likely to attract butterflies. Hometown nurseries are beginning to devote space to perennials and shrubs that will attract butterflies. One nursery in our area has taken this a step further and carries only plants that will benefit wildlife. Perhaps there is a nursery near you with a similar dedication to wildlife needs.

Some of the most useful and regionally focused resources to use to learn of butterfly nectar plants and larval foodplants are the regional butterfly gardening brochures being published by the North American Butterfly Association. They can be purchased singly or as a unit from NABA. *American Butterflies* and *Butterfly Gardening News,* both membership benefits of NABA, include insightful articles and tidbits on butterfly gardening from experts around the country. (See Further Information.)

Many nature centers now feature butterfly gardens and offer how-to workshops on gardening for wildlife. These formal programs are very valuable and can speed up your own learning curve dramatically. Any local or regional information is priceless. Geyata Ajilvsgi's terrific book *Butterfly Gardening for the South* is a must for gardeners living in Alabama, Florida, Georgia, North Carolina, South Carolina, Virginia, Tennessee, Louisiana, Mississippi, Arkansas, Oklahoma, and Texas. Actually, gardeners anywhere can learn a great deal from this book. Another gem is the "Desert Butterfly Gardening" brochure written by Jim Brock and published by the Arizona Native Plant Society and Sonoran Arthropod Studies Institute, which addresses gardening successfully in an extremely difficult and harsh environment.

Cardinal Rules of Plant Selection

There are some cardinal rules to follow that have benefited our butterfly garden and habitat and the gardens of friends. In your choice of plants, consider using as many native species as possible since they'll require less water, care, and fuss. At the same time be careful not to become such a native-plant purist that you overlook the many nonnative plants that are also excellent nectar sources. When selecting a nonnative plant always check to be sure it is not invasive — a plant that will readily spread beyond your yard. Always avoid invasive plants such as purple loosestrife, no matter how attractive they may seem to butterflies! Nurseries are aware of problems with loosestrife, and many are claiming no harm because they are selling sterile loosestrife plants. The sad reality, though, is that a sterile plant will develop seeds when visited by an insect that has also visited a fertile loosestrife, and there is so much loosestrife in the wild that this is inevitable.

Be very selective and choose plants most attractive to butterflies, then plant them in masses. A garden with one hundred different kinds of plants, one or two of each, is much less attractive to butterflies than massed plantings of well-selected plants. Fellow butterfly enthusiast and gardener Jane Ruffin calls the most heavily used nectar plants the "chocolate cakes." Be selective and make the irresistible "chocolate cakes" of your region the backbone of your garden.

Be sure to mix perennials and annuals. Perennials need to be planted only once; they live from year to year, with varying blooming periods. Over time many perennials need to be divided, providing you with new plants to stretch your gardens even farther into the yard or to give away to friends or acquaintances you're trying to convert into wildlife gardeners. Each of our perennials is marked with the friend's name who originally shared it with us and the date we received it — wonderful reminders of gifts that keep on giving. Annuals are short-lived plants; their entire life cycle takes place in one growing season. Many of them have a longer blooming period than perennials, and they can be tucked into bare spots in your perennial garden as filler. They often bloom right up until the frost. Our favorites in southern New Jersey include zinnias, Mexican sunflower, globe amaranth, scarlet sage, and scarlet milkweed. None of these is native, but they are also not invasive, so we've chosen to include them, and butterflies greatly benefit.

Another cardinal rule is to be sure to provide nectar from spring through late fall. This often means sparing some of your "weeds" that are spring bloomers. In the East wild mustards, purple dead-nettle, clover, dandelion, and common strawberry all attract spring butterflies. Include long-blooming nectar plants. In New Jersey butterfly bush fills this niche. It begins blooming in July and blooms right up through the first frost, some years into early November — a real bonus for migrating Monarchs and late-moving hummingbirds. Native to China, butterfly bush is a wonderful addition to the nonpurist's butterfly garden.

A garden that supplies only nectar forces butterflies to move on in search of larval foodplants. If you know the common butterflies of your area, look up their larval foodplants in a regional guide. Then consider doing a casual survey to find out how many of these plants you may already have in your yard. See which new ones you can tuck into your perennial flower beds or choose when planting a new tree, shrub, or vine.

Maybe you already have wild violets in the yard, the larval foodplant for fritillaries. Rather than remove them to make way for other plants, work around them, now knowing

they may be used by fritillaries for egg laying. Many gardeners are appalled when they find their parsley, dill, or fennel patch ravaged by large ornate green and black striped caterpillars. We purposefully intersperse large patches of fennel, parsley, and dill right into our perennial flower beds. The result, a yard full of newly emerged Black Swallowtails and still plenty of seasoning for the kitchen.

Larval foodplants for many butterfly species are grasses and weeds, plants we've all pulled out of our yards and gardens at one time or another, plants such as Queen Anne's lace, milkweed, lamb's quarters, curled dock, sweet everlasting, sheep sorrel, plantain, and clover. Learn to recognize the larval foodplants of local butterflies and moths. It may inspire a new respect for these plants and help you learn to tolerate and maybe even enjoy them in your yard. Leaving some edges unmowed may be all that is necessary to encourage these plants in your butterfly habitat.

Last, avoid the use of herbicides and pesticides. They're sure to affect the butterflies attracted to your garden. Quite often garden pests will be taken care of naturally in a healthy garden. An outbreak of aphids in our garden always draws in hungry lady bugs, whose larvae prey on aphids.

Complement Gardens with Unsavory Delights

Quite a few butterflies and moths have odd preferences and are attracted to feces, urine, sap, and rotten fruit. If you own dogs, do not be surprised to find butterflies on their droppings. Some of the more elusive butterflies find rotting fruit irresistible. Since we have no fruit trees in our yard, we buy pears, peaches, bananas, and watermelon to attract them. Watermelon is the easiest attractor; you simply place a flat slice on a plate and dole out new slices as the first dries out or gets moldy. Bananas have worked the best for us and they're always available, but they aren't always rotten enough to attract butterflies. We've learned to peel and freeze them; once thawed they are nice and liquidy and immediately attractive to butterflies. Our homemade butterfly feeder is nothing more than a ceramic plate with a lip (so liquids don't drip off), filled with gooey bananas and suspended from a tree by a simple plant hanger. We suspend it, rather than place it on the ground, so ants do not make off with the precious bananas. A little fresh orange juice each day keeps the bananas moist and attractive a while longer. We've enjoyed great looks at butterflies as they sip from our banana goo, including Red-spotted Purple, Red Admiral, Question Mark, Eastern Comma, Mourning Cloak, Common Wood-Nymph, Little Wood-Satyr, Appalachian Brown, Hackberry Emperor, and Tawny Emperor. At night a rich assortment of moths find it irresistible.

We're often asked about commercial butterfly feeders, the ones with a bottom compartment for sugar water and a perching area on top where butterflies can thrust their proboscis down into the sugar water. The only place we've seen these work is in southeastern Arizona, where they can be covered with Dull Firetips, a type of large skipper. In most areas these commercial butterfly feeders rarely work; butterflies seem totally uninterested.

Some butterflies are drawn to rotting fruit. This Red-spotted Purple is at a homemade butterfly feeder — a dish of gooey bananas.

You'll have far more luck making a homemade feeder like ours and using fruit.

A manmade or natural sandy opening in the garden, if wet down daily, may draw in puddling butterflies. We've laid the top to a birdbath on the ground and filled it with sand. On trips to the tropics and elsewhere, male butterfly researchers commonly urinate at a chosen spot, then return occasionally to see which butterflies have been attracted. Mammal urine has certain key minerals that attract puddling butterflies.

Maintaining Gardens

In southern New Jersey a killing frost wilts the last flowers in late October, and the parade of butterflies wanes. A few hardy species may be seen through November and into early December. The deep-freeze winter months seem endless without these entertaining gems. Just how butterflies survive the winter is important to understand because it relates directly to recommended gardening practices. As we've become more and more focused on gardening for butterflies, it has been a wonderful excuse to garden in a more relaxed fashion.

Most of our butterflies pass the winter not as an adult butterfly but as an egg on a plant, as a caterpillar in a curled-up leaf or down in the leaf litter, or as a chrysalis attached to a plant stem in a sheltered spot. For this reason we no longer tidy up the garden in the fall but leave the flower stalks standing. Not only do many birds feed on the seed heads and find safe cover in the garden through the winter, but this approach ensures the safety of the next generation of butterflies. Leaf raking, leaf blowing, burning, and mowing under trees once leaves have fallen are all a no-no in our yard. We stopped raking leaves when we learned that Luna Moths winter in their silken leaf-wrapped cocoons under sweetgum trees and that Hackberry Emperors winter as partially grown caterpillars in fallen leaves under hackberry trees. The too-tidy gardener is literally and physically bagging up and carting off next spring's butterflies and moths.

If you garden for butterflies, many "weeds" take on a new significance and are treated like prizes. The presence of unkempt areas near your formal gardens, where nature is given free rein, might contribute more than you think to your garden's success. As we have said, many weedy plants are essential larval foodplants for some of our favorite butterflies.

Actually, butterflies are an excellent excuse to spend less time fussing and more time enjoying the garden visitors. Sara Stein's excellent books *Noah's Garden* and *Planting Noah's Garden* wonderfully explain the ecological value of a more relaxed approach to gardening.

Through summer's heat we've found that mulching with grass clippings conserves water and keeps plants alive in our formal gardens. The grass is free, and it eventually breaks down into rich soil. An acquaintance with a lawn mowing service drops off six or so full trash cans and carts off the empty ones from the previous week. We smother unwanted weeds with grass clippings before they can crowd out perennials, and we surround newly planted annuals with it too.

The few species that winter as adult butterflies hibernate in protected crevices like those found in a woodpile.

How to Spot Butterflies

Visit natural meadows in your area to learn which nectar plants to incorporate into a meadow of your own. Migrating Monarchs on seaside goldenrod.

Create a Safe Hibernation Spot

A few species winter as adult butterflies, surviving the cold months by hibernating in protected crevices, inside woodpiles or stone walls, under shutters or shingles, inside hollow trees, or under loose tree bark. In the East these hardy butterflies include Question Mark, Eastern Comma, Compton Tortoiseshell, Mourning Cloak, and Red Admiral.

If you have a woodpile, it's likely that the few species that overwinter as adults may use it. If you don't, consider constructing one just for butterflies. Crisscross layers of logs to create lots of chambers. Place a layer of roofing shingles between the last two layers for the best protection from rain and snow. On a warm winter day you may find Mourning Cloaks or Compton Tortoiseshells lilting

about, but as soon as the temperature drops they'll return to their safe haven. These same few species might use a commercially sold butterfly house if few natural nooks and crannies are available. Unfortunately, the average person thinks butterfly houses will be used by lots of different butterfly species year-round. This is simply not true. Printed material with such misinformation often accompanies butterfly houses. They do no harm, but you should drastically limit your expectations.

Consider a Meadow

Now that you realize the value of grasses and weedy plants, consider incorporating a wildflower meadow into your butterfly habitat plan, even if it is as small as a flower bed. The easiest way to begin your meadow is to simply stop mowing. If the area has not been

Even a small wildflower meadow in your yard is beneficial to butterflies.

chemically treated, a rich diversity of plants, including a number of wildflowers, will come up in just the first year. You can speed things along by planting native wildflowers in your meadow. Asters, goldenrods, various milkweeds, and purple coneflower are all excellent choices. Denise Gibbs, a butterfly garden and meadow consultant in Maryland, recommends planting your wildflower seedlings or plugs in a wavy line or pattern so that when seeds disperse it looks the way it would in a natural meadow. If you live where uncut grass is unacceptable to your neighbors, make your meadow more pleasing by surrounding it with a low split-rail fence and place a sign at the entrance stating that the area is a "Wildflower Meadow for Butterflies." Of course the birds, bees, moths, and other critters will benefit too, but butterflies have a magical appeal. If your meadow is big enough, mow a winding walking path through it.

To keep your meadow a meadow it must be mowed once each year, preferably in the spring, otherwise woody shrubs and trees will seed there and eventually turn your meadow into a shrubby area and finally into a forest. As shrubs move in it becomes harder and harder to mow. It is important to do the mowing in the early spring, not in the fall, for a number of reasons: 1) the foot-high grasses and wildflower seed heads provide important cover and survival food to birds and other wildlife through the winter, and 2) many butterflies go through their life cycle (egg, caterpillar, chrysalis) tucked down in the weedy growth of your meadow. This being the case, rotation mowing ensures that some survive. In other words, mow half the meadow one spring and half the next spring. Use a nonmulching mower for the least impact possible; a sickle-bar mower does far less damage than a rotary brush-hog type and may even allow some survival of caterpillars and chrysalids.

Meadows and prairies are rare habitats today. Their creation and long-term maintenance, with butterflies in mind, varies considerably depending on where you live. Many of the resources included in Further Information are helpful.

Keep a Diary

Record the evolution of your yard into a butterfly habitat. Be sure to take photos from *Day One*. If you are new to gardening and you are about to dig up your carefully cared for lawn, record all the changes. Take photos from a variety of angles, making sure structures are in your photos as a reference. Record each season over a period of years with photos from these same angles. You will be amazed at the transformation. Visitors will want to know what it once looked like. The change will be so complete, so magical, that without a photo, they'll never believe you.

Keep a diary too. There is still so much to learn about butterfly nectar and larval foodplants. We can all make contributions by keeping good records of which nectar plants and larval foodplants are most attractive to butterflies in our own yards, when certain plants (including weeds) bloom, how early in the season or how late in the season they bloom, which butterflies come to which plants, and so much more.

How Quickly Can You Expect Results?

A first-year butterfly garden can be instantly successful, luring in butterflies and other pollinators from near and afar. It all depends on your surroundings. Butterflies need to come from somewhere, so you need some natural habitat nearby that has not had heavy uses of herbicides and pesticides and is not overly controlled and managed. Be patient, though, as gardens do get better over time.

Our own gardens are on a small lot, just shy of a half acre, in a rural area of New Jersey. As a random test we did a "lunch-hour" count there one August 6th, and in one hour we saw about 30 individuals of 12 species: Eastern Tiger Swallowtail,

Spicebush Swallowtail, Cabbage White, Red-banded Hairstreak, Summer Azure, American Snout, Red Admiral, Common Wood Nymph, Monarch, Silver-spotted Skipper, Broad-winged Skipper, and Hayhurst's Scallopwing. All were regulars except for the scallopwing, an uncommon species and a good find.

Two hours later we saw four additional species: Red-spotted Purple, Least Skipper, Sachem, and Zabulon Skipper. Around 6:00 P.M., we saw five Eastern Tailed Blues (mysteriously absent earlier in the day, possibly just emerged), giving us 17 species for our daily list — an average day. The count wasn't helped by the weather, since high cumulus clouds covered the sun during about half the lunch-hour period, or by the many dragonflies, including the rapacious swamp darner seen

A Hayhurst's Scallopwing attracted to heliotrope in a planted butterfly garden.

Suttons' garden *(left)* **after 12 years and the Watsons' garden** *(right)* **in its third year.**

patrolling. In our favor was the fact that this is a long-established garden (about 12 years old) that is constantly nurtured.

Additional monitoring or an all-day vigil would probably have added Orange Sulphur, 'Olive' Juniper Hairstreak, Question Mark, American Lady, and Dun Skipper — all seen during the previous two days — giving us possibly 22 species. Twenty-four species is our record daily count, obtained in early July when native common milkweed and planted bee balm are at their peak blooming period — a time that corresponds with peak butterfly diversity.

Compared to the random count in the Sutton yard, a look the next day at Dale Watson's garden, about two miles away, produced a remarkably similar species list but about three times as many individuals. The Watson yard is larger, with a larger garden and more open-space sunny areas needed by butterflies. It is also near the saltmarsh upland edge, which no doubt entices many migrant butterflies to

stop and nectar. The Watsons' yard was remarkable with nearly 90 butterflies — a blizzard of action and color on a bright summer afternoon. Most remarkable though is that this butterfly garden is only three years old — living proof that satisfaction and results, if not instantaneous, are achievable in the short term from butterfly gardening.

For a geographical comparison, Sheri Williamson conducted a lunch-hour count in her garden the same day, August 7, in Bisbee, Arizona (south of Tucson, near Sierra Vista). She saw 27 individuals of 17 species: Southern Dogface, Cloudless Sulphur, Lyside Sulphur, Sleepy Orange, Tailed Orange, Ceraunus Blue, Gulf Fritillary, Variegated Fritillary, Queen, Arizona Skipper, Northern Cloudywing, Acacia Skipper, Common Sootywing, Orange Skipperling, Fiery Skipper, Bronze Roadside-Skipper, and Nysa Roadside-Skipper.

Here also, it was a random count and considered average for this two-year-old garden.

How to Spot Butterflies

Nectar plants that attracted these butterflies included *Lantana camara*, a hybrid *Lantana*, *Verbena tenuisecta*, butterfly bush, *Salvia farinacea*, *Salvia coccinea*, wild sunflower, garden zinnia, canna, *Erigeron divergens*, and Texas ranger (*Leucophyllum* sp.). In southeastern Arizona, this count was prior to the well-known late-summer time of peak diversity that results from the benefits of the rainy season and the numerous vagrant species from Mexico. A count later in the season would have been higher. But the point of this exercise was to show what numbers and variety a well-established home butterfly garden might attract. While you cannot judge your absolute enjoyment by numbers alone, we can only attest that our garden makes for a highly enjoyable place to spend our lunch hour or a day off. Some early risers such as swallowtails can often be seen before the workday begins (as soon as the sun hits the garden) and others, particularly fruit-feeding species such as Hackberry Emperors, Red-spotted Purple, and Question Mark, can often be seen until near sundown. A butterfly garden can be a wonderful way to bring nature, education, and enjoyment to your yard — and on a daily basis. Results may vary, but you *can* try gardening in your own space. If you do not own property, get involved in a community garden on public lands.

A passion for butterfly gardening has swept across the United States; one can only hope it's in the nick of time. Thousands upon thousands of acres of butterfly habitat throughout our country have been lost. The fallow fields and prairies full of wildflowers and grasses of yesteryear have become harder, if not impossible, to find. Many childhood memories consist of days spent chasing after butterflies through such fields. Many of these fields are gone and with them the butterflies. Today, wide strips along road shoulders are mowed to stubble weekly during the growing season. Efforts in Texas — and in a limited way in other states — to plant and encourage wildflowers along roadways are excellent, but they can happen none too soon for butterflies. Millions of lawns are treated by lawn-care companies so that nary a dandelion is spared — and dandelions in some parts of the country offer nectar to spring butterflies long before our butterfly gardens are even peeking through the ground. Corporate properties with sprawling sod lawns cover thousands of acres in some states. These green deserts have taken the place of fallow farm fields and wildflower meadows. Thankfully, a few corporations are "going wild" and turning part or all of their sod lawn back into meadows. Even some well-intentioned gardeners do not understand the big picture. They plant gardens full of butterfly flowers but simultaneously spray poisons on aphids and other bugs; weed out important host plants; and manicure the garden endlessly, carting off eggs, caterpillars, and chrysalises . . . the next generation of butterflies.

We hope that backyard butterfly gardens will ignite the imagination of many, and efforts will trickle over into classrooms as well as planning decisions throughout the country. Optimistically, efforts will be in time to benefit our butterflies, many of which are confined to limited remaining natural wild areas, habitat that is diminishing day by day.

Butterfly Conservation

THE DAY WAS YET YOUNG, but the July sun was beginning to burn away the morning mist in the valley meadows beyond. As we climbed the stairs to the barracks-style office, we squinted from the sun's reflection on the whitewashed walls. The building was dated but immaculately kept. Jim Dowdell, a fellow butterfly enthusiast, had joined us to visit a military base in central Pennsylvania, the holy grail of eastern North American butterflying. We were here to see the last remaining colony of Regal Fritillaries left in the East, a dream of many years.

"Mornin', Butterfly Lady," the sergeant on duty behind the desk said as he smiled familiarly at our host, Barb Barton, a tall and easygoing zoologist with The Nature Conservancy. "Going up to check on your bugs?" he joked. "Sure thing," answered Barb. "These folks are here to help with the census," she added. The sergeant, who had been signing Barb in on the visitor's log for several years, said, "Should be a good day for it . . . let me call up there and get you clearance." As we showed our credentials and signed in, however, the military radio crackled with devastating news, "We got some fast movers inbound and hot . . . ETA 0840. I can't have no visitors now." Barb quickly explained the military jargon, "Fast movers are jets, probably F-16s. Hot means using live ammo on the firing range — which is near where we're going."

The disappointment on our faces must

Saving imperiled Regal Fritillary habitat, such as this remnant Pennsylvania prairie *(above)*, is a major conservation struggle. Many species such as the Red-banded Hairstreak *(right)*, benefit from enlightened land management.

have been palpable. The predawn departure and five-hour drive were immaterial, but the chance that we would miss seeing the Regals was a bitter disappointment.

"Hold on," said the friendly sergeant. "Let me check the schedule." A check of the books and another radio call revealed, "If you can just wait 20 minutes or so, that's the last live firing scheduled today." Relief flooded through us. Twenty minutes was no hardship!

As we waited for the red flags to be lowered on the range, Barb enthusiastically filled us in on the biology of the Regal Fritillary and detailed the intense conservation efforts to protect them. Orange and purple-black above, chocolate-fudge brown with white splashes below, the Regal Fritillary lives up to its name. Large, nearly Monarch-size, and striking, the Regal Fritillary was once found from New Brunswick west to the Dakotas. Declining in the East since the 1950s, there is only one surviving colony left east of Illinois. Its disappearance is only partially explained by the loss of eastern grasslands to intensive agriculture and housing, since they are gone from a number of seemingly unchanged areas where they were once found. "They may be an indicator species — a canary in a coal mine, as it were," ventured Barb.

In the midwestern prairies, Regal Fritillaries remain common in some areas, although they are declining in others. "No surprise! Habitat loss is the biggest problem," Ann Swengel, who studies them on Wisconsin prairies, had explained during a recent workshop. "Open space has changed — habitats are much altered and reduced from the days when Bison and Pronghorn roamed freely on prairies." Today, protection, management, and prairie restoration play a major role in the conservation of the Regal Fritillary.

"Let's work through here," Barb said, as she began her census route. We entered the field with tally-clickers in hand. "Watch where you step though, there's live ordnance all through here," warned Barb. We walked *very* carefully, following Barb and stepping only in open areas. A nectaring butterfly soon caught our eye. It was a fritillary, but the wrong one — a Great Spangled Fritillary, usually a good find, but playing only a supporting role today. We flushed sulphurs and Cabbage Whites, and as the morning warmed, swallowtails became active — four different species: Tiger, Spicebush, Black, and Pipevine. "We're getting into the good area," said Barb just moments before an ethereal vision floated out of the nearby grasses and paused to nectar on butterfly weed — a Regal Fritillary, one of the largest and most dramatic of all North American butterflies, and our first ever! Somehow Ann Swengel's apt description came to mind, "prairie royalty!"

Soon there were several, then our count reached into the dozens. They were active — males particularly — patrolling rapidly, disappearing over the gently rolling grassland horizons, dipping into swales. Some were cooperative enough for photographs and lengthy looks as we drank in their magnificent colors and patterns.

Barb's enthusiasm was infectious as she proudly showed off her charges. As the temperature climbed, she removed her long-sleeved jacket to reveal an immaculate and tasteful tattoo of a Regal Fritillary gracing her

The Regal Fritillary lives up to its name. Large — nearly Monarch-size — and striking, it was once found from New Brunswick west to the Dakotas.

shoulder — a symbol of her love for this beleaguered species and her total commitment to its conservation. "The entire population here inhabits this series of old fields — but it's only about a six-mile by one-half-mile area in all," explained Barb. Inadvertently, the military has

managed for the Regal Fritillary. Periodic maneuvers keep the land open. Fires resulting from artillery practice and bombing create the fire ecology necessary for the prairielike habitat, composed of native grasses and shrubs, to endure. "They wouldn't be here without the military — otherwise it would become successional and grow into forest," explained Barb. Also, because the area is off-limits to the general public, butterfly collectors — who still create problems for many species in some areas — can't get in. "There are dangers though," Barb cautioned. "The military has plans to open some of this area to increased maneuvers; that could be devastating. It takes full-time vigilance." It was the old conservation adage and lament: you have to save an endangered species over and over again.

By late afternoon the July heat dissipated and we returned happily to the car, steeped in Regal Fritillaries and their imperiled Pennsylvania prairie. There was time for one more bit of wonder. Always indefatigable, Jim checked a bog near the road and spotted an immaculate Baltimore Checkerspot nectaring on knapweed. Fairly common in their single brief flight period, Baltimores are inextricably linked to turtlehead, their host plant, and are, therefore, highly localized in their distribution. It was our thirty-first species for the day, a butterfly list that included an amazing five species of fritillaries — including Aphrodite and Silver-bordered (also becoming rare in many parts of the East). The Regal Fritillary count for the day? More than 60. "It's early in their flight period, but it looks to be a good year," Barb offered encouragingly.

Not only was Barb Barton's enthusiasm contagious, but she showed an upbeat optimism rarely found in those who study disappearing species. It wasn't necessarily a fervent hope for the Regal Fritillaries at their last stronghold, but a confidence that there is still the chance, that it is proper and just to be doing the right thing, that in the conviction is the potential and satisfaction. The day left many lasting impressions, including a reaffirmation of the enduring need for Lepidoptera conservation. But the abiding memory is of Barb Barton, striding long-legged across lush meadows, embodying butterfly protection, chasing, counting — and conserving — prairie royalty.

Threats to Butterflies

If we are to have plenty of butterflies to spot and enjoy, we must preserve and protect them. A great deal has been written about butterfly conservation, but the bulk of this has been done in the United Kingdom. They are leagues ahead of North America in recognizing the importance of butterflies and in conserving their habitats. Throughout Britain, the British Butterfly Conservation Society has long been dedicated to saving wild butterflies and their habitats. Many butterfly preserves have been established, but their chief focus remains the ensuring of proper management of private lands, meadows, moors, and heaths. In the United States, few state nongame and endangered species programs have even begun the process of recognizing troubled Lepidoptera, and in most cases true protection is probably decades away.

The principal threat to butterfly populations in the United States, to vastly oversimplify it, is the loss of habitat. This takes many forms. A reversal of our nationwide trend to convert fields and farms to malls, shopping centers, and strip development may well take a change of attitude and values, but butterfly conservation can take place on many levels, locally and even in our own yards.

In the East, with the inexorable march of civilization, much of the future of butterflies lies in the creation of additional protected lands and in the management of existing open space — state and local parks, state wildlife management areas (WMA), and national wildlife refuges (NWR). Some are excellent in their current configuration, others are managed inappropriately for butterflies.

In some state game lands and WMAs, we have been appalled to see beautiful fallow fields, full of nectar and host plants, mowed flat in early summer, killing grassland birds and butterflies alike (in one case, just two days before a 4th of July Butterfly Count was to occur there). When asked why, game managers replied, "We've got to get these fields ready for the pheasant release in November." A one-time mowing, at a better time in late winter or early spring, could have allowed for a myriad of other species, including butterflies, to raise numerous generations. Urge improvement and multispecies nongame management in your area. Alternate mowing of patches, every other year, ensures that some butterflies will survive in unmowed patches to repopulate the mowed patches.

Corporate lawns require huge amounts of chemicals to remain lush and green well into the fall when native grasses have turned soft shades of gold, brown, and tan. These unnatural monocultures, often former fields, offer no cover and no food to wildlife, including butterflies. Corporations that are turning lawns back into grassy wildflower meadows are to be commended and encouraged, even showcased.

Roadside mowing can be disastrous to butterflies. One September day, we found hundreds of individuals of 21 species along rich roadsides near the Delaware Bay, all nectaring on stands of seaside goldenrod, Joe-pye-weed (blooming late because of an earlier mowing), and ironweed. Monarchs were abundant, including dozens of caterpillars feeding on lavish milkweed. Three days later, we led a field trip to the area and found that the highway department had mowed. Actually, they had not just mowed the road shoulders but they had cut back with a vengeance some 30 feet to agricultural fields, and they had even mowed down the inside edge of ditches all the way down to the water. It was a scorched-earth policy. No nectar was left anywhere on the 5,000-acre tract! We could find only eight butterflies of three species where just three days before there had been hundreds of butterflies.

Thousands, if not millions, of Monarchs are killed outright as eggs, caterpillars, and chrysalises as roadside stands of milkweed are mowed through the summer and fall. In your area, urge responsible, wildlife-friendly mowing. Perhaps through local schools, teach road crews what milkweed is and have them lift the blade when coming to milkweed patches and other stands of wildflowers. Better yet, ask for a once-a-year mowing schedule, in which mowing is withheld until wildflowers go to seed; a late-winter mowing lets the seeds disperse and allows the standing plants to provide food and cover through the winter for birds and other wildlife. Such a simple, common-sense decision will promote native wildflowers and butterflies. You will be met with the standard "safety first" response, yet there is little need for 20–30-foot-wide mowed swaths along little-traveled country roads, except maybe on blind curves.

Happily, roadside mowing is diminishing in many areas as targeted native wildflower programs take over. Texas has the model program, with roadsides ablaze with color in season. Don't be surprised in Texas when a random roadside stop produces many and varied butterflies — all because of the wildflower protection policy.

Pesticides and herbicides have drastic impacts on butterfly populations. The days of DDT were not so very long ago, when much more than intended victims were impacted. We have come so far, but still choose the easy solution at the expense of unintended victims. In New Jersey, some areas of intensive modern agriculture are almost devoid of butterflies, partly because no fields are left fallow, but also because so many pesticides and herbicides are used. The relatively new and highly touted no-till agricultural practices and policies often only increase herbicide use. In Connecticut, widespread aerial gypsy moth spraying has, according to the late Roger Tory Peterson, virtually eliminated silk moths in much of the state, and a lot of butterflies too. In Florida, widespread aerial application of Malathion for adult mosquito control has "controlled" many butterflies as well. In Massachusetts, a butterfly count was done along a powerline cut one day before an aerial spray of Malathion (for mosquito control): 109 butterflies of 12 species were found. A count two days after the spraying found four individuals of three species. In New Jersey, in our own yard, 54 individuals of 13 species were seen the day before an aerial spraying of Malathion for mosquito control (five passes by helicopter). The following day, five individuals of five species were seen. While one spraying may not have lasting long-term effects, repeated spraying can and will. In short, most chemicals and butterflies don't mix. Urge against unnecessary spraying in your area — particularly "make work"–type spraying ("use up the spray or we'll lose the money in the budget").

One area in which we have seen improvement, at least in our region, is in the use of herbicides in powerline and railroad right-of-ways (ROWs). Enlightenment has led to the replacement of spraying with mowing in many areas. Where once ROWs were brown lifeless dead zones, they are now filled with weedy vegetation, wildflowers, and butterflies. Because of the ecotones created, edges where habitat types come together, ROWs remain one of the best butterfly-finding areas, with numbers far higher than in adjacent uniform habitat. Urge responsible mowing rather than spraying of all ROWs, roadsides, railways, and pipeline and transmission lines. Properly managed, they can be among the *best* butterfly hotspots.

Much of butterfly conservation is just plain common sense. One landowner (of 21 acres) told us, "I never see many butterflies," despite a perennial garden and several butterfly bushes. A look around told the story: an oversized "requisite" green lawn, borders repeatedly treated with herbicide "to keep the stone walls from growing up with weeds," and overgrazed pastures treated regularly to "get rid of that awful pesky thistle." There just wasn't much butterfly habitat, nectar or host plants, on that gentleman's farm.

Healthy butterfly populations and chemicals just don't mix. We never use chemicals in our yard. Despite weeds in the driveway and the raised eyebrow of a neighbor, we refuse to use chemicals. Pull weeds by hand. If you need a lawn (and so do we — for our dogs and as a walkway through the gardens), don't treat it with all kinds of chemicals. Remember, the modern model green lawn is a monotypic-habitat dead zone. Instead, spread clover on the grass and don't cut it as often. You might be amazed at the Eastern Tailed Blues and sulphurs using the clover, both as nectar and as their host plant. Leave the dandelions. One of the most curious of American attitudes is the disdain of the dandelion. To us, it is a beautiful wildflower, a splash of color before much else is in bloom, and an early season nectar source for butterflies when little else is available.

While leading a butterfly walk in Cape May Point's public butterfly garden we were distracted by a young child snatching at nectaring Monarchs and other butterflies. The child's parent was there too, also "bagging" live butterflies. Upon gentle but firm questioning of their intentions, we learned that the child's teacher had assigned the class to make a butterfly collection. This parent had heard about Monarchs gathering at Cape May and decided to partake — no matter that they were doing so in a garden, a haven established by a community proud of its migrating Monarchs. Unfortunately this was not a lone case; residents and friends had seen a number of other parent-child teams bagging Monarchs and other butterflies — all to be killed, mounted, presented to the teacher, and eventually to be forgotten.

No one has the right to enter a public garden established as a butterfly sanctuary and plunder it. To encourage a child to perform such a negative act can instill long-term disregard for butterflies and other living creatures. Sadly, there are countless butterflies hit by cars every day. If a collection must be made to teach about species, butterfly parts, variation in size, etc., why not direct children to look on their car grill for dead butterflies or (accompanied by an adult) to gather road-killed butterflies from a road shoulder. There is no reason to take a live butterfly that has survived so many hurdles and cut its life short for a soon-to-be-forgotten collection. It is amazing to us that some teachers still make such assignments. If you are a teacher or are in a position to guide your child's or grandchild's teacher, we strongly suggest that instead of a bug collection consider having the students plant a schoolyard butterfly garden of nectar and host plants. Such a garden could act as an outdoor classroom. Student assignments then would entail developing observation skills — have them keep a diary and conduct mini research projects or art projects. Students could observe butterfly-plant relationships, dependence of certain species on certain host plants, life cycles, effects of weather on activity, and much more. Such a learning opportunity is positive, and the butterflies live on to entertain and teach others. Such an assignment also carries a strong conservation message. Perhaps the child will plant a butterfly garden at home and so teach family members and others. There is nothing so positive as opening a child's eyes to the study of live butterflies that will naturally come to and depend on a garden the child has planted.

Large-scale releases of captive-raised butterflies, often Painted Ladies and Monarchs, at weddings and other special occasions are becoming more and more popular. Well-intentioned people may think they are benefiting the environment, but in reality such releases are highly unnatural. Releases often place butterflies where they would not naturally be found. Releases occur in all seasons, so they are likely to release butterflies when they cannot possibly survive, and the butterflies die a heartless death. While some of the butterflies sold for such releases have been raised on butterfly farms or ranches in captivity, others have been stolen during raids on butterfly sanctuaries, such as the sensitive Monarch winter roosts. Because there is a demand and because each butterfly might fetch $10 for such a release, the number of raids on butterfly preserves will only increase. Releases may also be responsible for or contribute to the spread of disease. Some of the ranched butterflies carry fungal disease. When released, they may spread disease to healthy wild populations. Another problem with butterfly releases is that they muddle reality. Painted Lady numbers fluctuate dramatically in the North. Very few or none might be seen following a winter when freezing temperatures reach into our southern states. School classes raising kits of Painted Ladies and releasing them into the wild sometimes release Painted Ladies where no wild ones have been seen because of a bad winter. With so many schools now raising and releasing Painted Ladies, it is hard to know how the wild population is faring.

Monarchs, being highly migratory, are faced with many gauntlets. Logging in Mexico at and near the Monarch overwintering roosts is frightening to see, but they are threatened throughout the rest of North America too by loss of habitat (housing developments, agricultural expansion) and the increasing use of herbicides that not only eliminates milkweed plants for egg laying, but also destroys many nectar plants needed by adult butterflies. We can all make a difference by speaking up. We can allow common milkweed to grow in our meadows. And we can plant swamp milkweed, butterfly weed, and scarlet milkweed — or whatever native milkweeds occur in the area — in our gardens. Indeed, we can garden for Monarchs by planting milkweed and by sharing our knowledge of their needs with a friend, who may share it with another friend, and another, and another — maybe creating a path of milkweed from Mexico to Canada and back for Monarchs. Butterfly conservation is needed and can occur on many levels. But, as is true with so many forms of conservation, it starts at home. So much of Lepidoptera conservation is just common sense.

PART TWO

Butterflies of North America

Butterflies of North America

THE FIRST BUTTERFLIES most people see are the big showy ones, like Monarchs, swallowtails, or the large fritillaries. They are hard to overlook since they are widespread and rather common butterflies with wingspans ranging from 2½ inches to 5½ inches. Once the spotter's attention is caught by the big and showy butterflies, another world is within reach. The same garden or wildflower meadow with the bright orange Monarch flitting from flower head to flower head also holds a plethora of tiny and easily overlooked butterflies. Many of the blues, hairstreaks, and elfins are not much bigger than a thumbnail when they perch closed-winged on the ground or on a flower. Many of the metalmarks and coppers are also tiny even when they perch with their wings open, as they commonly do. Many of the skippers are nondescript and quite small. The reality is that most butterflies are small and easily overlooked, but just as beautiful and sometimes even more breathtaking than the large butterflies that first catch the eye.

Spotting butterflies will be far more satisfying once you have an understanding of the different groups of butterflies you may encounter. To identify a butterfly it is imperative to first place it in one of the groupings — this is the system on which virtually all identification guides are based.

The 717 species of butterflies that occur in North America, north of Mexico, can generally be divided into seven separate groups, or families, according to their structure. The visual characteristics most often used to separate one family from another are usually the configuration of the wing veins, the coloration, and how the butterfly sits, or perches. Some groups almost always perch with their wings open, others with them usually closed. Patterns or markings of butterflies — different species' variation of lines, spots, and patches of color — can be misleading at times because of similarities, overlap, and mimicking among species and groups. With some practice, though, the general structure or look of a butterfly is usually sufficient to place it in the proper family — an important first step in the identification process which should work anywhere in North America. (This often does *not* work in the tropics, however, where mimicry is far more common.) With a little experience you will find that each family of butterflies has its own GISS (or "Jizz," as it has become known): General Impression, Shape, and Size.

SWALLOWTAILS
PAPILIONIDAE

Most swallowtails have tailed hindwings, like this Zebra Swallowtail.

Swallowtails are found throughout North America. About 31 of the 600 species found worldwide occur in the United States. Some of the largest and most dramatic of all butterflies are swallowtails. Some are quite common; others, because of their size and beauty, have become threatened thanks to collectors. The Schaus' Swallowtail, found in the Florida Keys, is highly endangered, mainly because of habitat loss and degradation.

Swallowtails are large butterflies with wingspans ranging from about 2½ inches to over 5 inches. They are bright and distinctive butterflies usually with tailed hindwings. A few do not have tails, such as Polydamas Swallowtail and Ruby-spotted Swallowtail, and on some species the tails are barely noticeable, such as Short-tailed Swallowtail and Indra Swallowtail. It is believed that swallowtail tails, often in combination with colorful spots near the base of the tails, confuse potential predators by resembling antennae. This back-to-front mimicry, or the illusion of a dummy head and antennae on the posterior end, is a survival strategy of swallowtails wherein birds mistakenly try to capture the wrong end and get nothing more than a mouthful of wing, allowing the butterfly to escape with its body still intact. While afield you will notice butterflies missing chunks of their wings — sometimes in the perfect shape of a bird's beak! Swallowtails can also lose their tails to simple wear and tear, and to vegetation that brushes against them while they are perched or nectaring.

Many swallowtail caterpillars resemble bird droppings. This interesting mimicry is a survival technique — the caterpillar "disappears" on a branch or leaf and is overlooked by the hungry eyes of potential predators, from predatory wasps to insect-eating birds. Later instars of many swallowtail caterpillars resemble a snake with two large false eyespots, another mimicry survival technique. In temperate North America, most species spend the winter in the chrysalis stage. In tropical areas of Florida, Texas, and Arizona, they are multibrooded, and adult butterflies might be encountered any month of the year.

Swallowtails, because of their size and bright colors, are one of the easiest groups to spot. They are the first butterflies many of us become aware of in our gardens and while afield. In early spring, before lush wildflowers are abundant, most swallowtails are spotted on the move, dashing by as they search for nectar or a mate. As summer unfolds and gardens, roadsides, and fallow fields come into bloom, lush stands of favorite nectar sources concentrate swallowtails and many other butterflies. Day lilies lining roadsides, Turk's-cap lilies in wet meadows, lone wood lilies in sun-dappled woodlands, and lilies in formal gardens all draw in swallowtails. Pickerelweed and buttonbush on pond and stream edges are also favorites with swallowtails. Field and roadside stands of various milkweeds, thistles, *Eupatoriums,* bee balm, asters, sunflowers, and goldenrods are also magnets to these large and showy butterflies. Butterfly gardens planted with many of these favorite perennials and complemented with lantana, pentas, sedum, zinnias, verbenas, and butterfly bush will surely draw swallowtails right into your own yard for study and enjoyment.

Learn to recognize specific host plants in your area and you are sure to find the swallowtails that depend on them. In southern New Jersey, a dark swallowtail fluttering around a sassafras tree can only be a female Spicebush Swallowtail preparing to lay eggs. Hercules' club in South Carolina and lemon and lime trees in Florida almost always have Giant Swallowtails in attendance. A wet meadow full of water parsnip is sure to draw in Black Swallowtails. A little bit of host plant knowledge will save you lots of time randomly searching. Just about every gardener is likely to attract Black Swallowtails by simply planting parsley, fennel, dill, carrot, Queen Anne's lace, celery, or rue. One need only remember to plant enough for both the table and Black Swallowtail caterpillars.

While afield, also look for swallowtails at puddles, seeps, and streamsides. They readily puddle and are one of the most likely butterflies to be found at sources of moisture.

Swallowtails are less dependent on sun and high temperatures than most other groups of butterflies are. In the Northeast, Tiger and Spicebush Swallowtails (along with Monarchs) often nectar and fly on cloudy days. Swallowtails are usually among the first to be active in the morning and the last to linger in the evening. On crisp spring mornings, as soon as the first rays of sunlight reach the garden, we have enjoyed Eastern Tiger Swallowtails. Because of their size, swallowtails may retain enough heat to be less solar-dependent than other groups.

Despite being large and easily spotted, swallowtails can sometimes be hard to get a good look at. Many continually flap their wings while nectaring, making critical observation and photography quite difficult.

How to Spot Butterflies

WHITES AND SULPHURS
PIERIDAE

Like the swallowtails, the **whites** and **sulphurs** are a cosmopolitan family, with about 700 species of whites and more than 300 species of sulphurs found worldwide. They show their greatest diversity in the tropics. There are 22 species of whites and 37 kinds of sulphurs in the United States and Canada, ranging from south Texas to Arctic treeline. Most Pierids are medium-sized butterflies, though a few are small and some are huge.

Whites are generally white and sulphurs are usually yellow or orange, but there are exceptions. Female Cloudless Sulphurs can be quite white in summer and fall. Female Orange Sulphurs and Clouded Sulphurs may be white (form *alba*). Most Pierids show spotting in the wings: black in whites and reddish in sulphurs. Some are sexually dimorphic, the males having different patterns, generally flashier, and therefore separable from females. Some of the more tropical Pierids are seasonally dimorphic as well, with spring individuals being more heavily marked. Many Pierids are migratory or at least irruptive, and large undirectional movements are sometimes noted. Most Pierids are strong fliers and move in a straight, steady path. Sulphurs usually bask in sunlight with the wings closed, turning sideways to the sun. Whites usually bask this way but sometimes partially open their wings. Male Pierids commonly patrol to find females.

Whites are usually not too hard to spot. Look for them in open country. Pastures and hayfields are usually a good bet. Their caterpillars feed mainly on members of the Mustard family, therefore disturbed areas and fallow fields can be excellent, for this is where many mustards grow.

Sulphur caterpillars feed on various clovers and beans in the Pea family. Agricultural areas, particularly hayfields and pastures, are good spots to find them. Also check puddles, since

Usually whites are white (Cabbage White, *left*) and sulphurs yellow (Clouded Sulphur).

freshly emerged male Pierids often participate in ground puddling at damp patches, mostly during the heat of the day.

Pierids can be found in most habitats and throughout the butterfly season, spring through fall, since many are continuously brooded. In much of the country they are among the most abundant species, from eastern meadows to western prairies. The Orange Sulphur, formerly called the Alfalfa Butterfly, is one of the most common butterflies throughout much of the United States, being multibrooded and occurring in most open areas. Farm areas with extensive alfalfa fields twinkle as hundreds of Orange Sulphurs dash about after one another. Some whites, such as the orangetips which fly only in early spring, are single-brooded with a finite flight period. The alert spotter can intercept patrolling male orangetips by quietly waiting for one to return along its route.

The Cabbage White, generally common — particularly in the East — is a nonnative species that may have had an impact on native whites in some areas. This Eurasian butterfly was introduced into Quebec about 1860, and by 1881, it was found throughout the entire eastern United States. It is now found throughout the country and can be abundant, particularly around towns and disturbed areas. It is multibrooded (except in the far northern part of its range) and is usually one of the first butterflies of spring and a lingerer into late autumn. The Cabbage White's larval foodplant is any member of the Cabbage family: cabbage, broccoli, cauliflower . . . hence, they are abundant and a pest to farmers.

While not as spectacular in color and pattern as many other groups, the whites and sulphurs are a significant part of our butterfly fauna, bringing color to vacant lots and desert alike. They catch the eye and can be very easy to spot, or they can be maddeningly difficult to get good looks at because of their rapid, direct flight. One might see more than a hundred Cloudless Sulphurs dash by before one of them pauses to nectar. The migratory and irruptive nature of sulphurs arouses interest among butterfly watchers throughout the country. In northern states, watchers eagerly anticipate sulphur invasions from the South — from the tiny Little Yellow to the huge Cloudless Sulphur.

COPPERS, HAIRSTREAKS, AND BLUES
(LYCAENIDAE)

This group, sometimes known as the gossamer-wing butterflies, is a very large family of tiny butterflies, ranging in size from ⅞ inches to 2 inches. Many are quite beautiful but often overlooked because of their size. Close-focus binoculars are a must to enjoy these tiny gems. Worldwide, this is the largest family of butterflies, with more than 4,700 species known, and with some still being discovered and described! There are about 135 species in North America, occurring from the subtropics (places like Florida, Texas, Arizona, and southern California) to the Arctic.

Coppers are found worldwide, but are mainly found in Europe and North America. Of about 55 species worldwide, 16 are found in the United States and Canada. Adults are

Most coppers, such as this Tailed Copper, are western species.

often coppery in color but some are brown, blue, or gray above. Many species are usually associated with moist meadows or bogs. In the United States, most coppers are western species, with only four found in the Northeast. The American Copper is widely distributed. Look for it in disturbed open areas. The Bronze Copper is rare and localized in the Northeast, but growing more common in the West. The yellowish Bog Copper, an obligate bog species, is never found away from acidic cranberry bogs, where it nectars at cranberry flowers and lays its eggs on cranberry, its larval foodplant. During its brief two-week flight period many hundreds might be seen in a day, but never more than a few yards from their bog habitat. Because many coppers have just one flight and because of their spectacular intricate patterns, coppers are usually a prize find for the butterfly spotter.

Most **hairstreaks** usually show, at least when freshly emerged, very fine tails on their hindwings. These hair-thin tails, plus streaks of white or brown on the hindwing, give this group their name. Hairstreaks commonly perch with closed wings, but move the wings back and forth, causing the tails to rub together. It is thought that this behavior may shift the attention of birds and other predators to the eyespot coloration and the antenna-like tails, causing them to strike at the wrong end of the potential meal.

There are about 2,000 hairstreaks worldwide; more than half of them are found in the American tropics. About 80 hairstreaks are found in North America, north of Mexico. Some have many flights (broods), some just one; therefore, some are easy to spot, others are very seasonal and more difficult to see. In some years there are large numbers of hairstreaks, while during other years they can be scarce. Such variations in numbers are not well known or easily understood — they are probably linked to climate, including temperature and rainfall variation. For some early season butterflies, a late frost that kills emerging leaves can have a devastating effect on newly hatched caterpillars, which need the leaves for food. If the first brood is thus affected there are few adults, fewer eggs, and a greatly reduced second brood as well. In the East, it seems that hairstreak numbers generally show greater yearly variation than any other group of butterflies.

To find hairstreaks, learn their daily activity patterns. Most hairstreaks treetop or hilltop for part of the day, the males seeking elevated perches to await females. In the West, many hairstreaks seek slopes or cliffs, often traveling some distance from where they were hatched. Butterfly watchers should seek hair-streaks in such places particularly during mid-day. Search for them at nectar sources early in the day and again in late afternoon.

Elfins, as their name implies, are a group of tiny hairstreaks with a single flight in early spring. Most are rich brown in color, and binoculars are essential to bring out their intricate patterns. They are usually found in woodlands. Look for them in sunny glades along woodland roads. They can be found basking and puddling on the road as soon as the sun warms up the road surface. One of the best ways to spot elfins is to walk gravel roads, flushing elfins as you go. Be alert for any movement, follow it with your eyes, and when it lands on the road surface ahead have your binoculars ready. During the chill of early spring, midday heat is best. Look for areas out of the wind. While some elfins seek sunny perches low or on the ground, others treetop, and some, such as Eastern and Western Pine Elfins, perch on small pines and nearby shrubs awaiting females. Because of the vagaries of spring weather, elfins have a protracted flight period, even though they are single-brooded. Individual male Brown Elfins have been known to live for more than two weeks in the wild. If you hit the peak of their emergence, they can be numerous, and their whirling frenetic courtship flights are exuberant — a hallmark of spring and a harbinger of things to come for the vernal butterfly watcher.

Blues are found worldwide, but mainly in northern temperate regions. About 32 species are recognized in the United States and Canada, although what comprises our species concept is rapidly being reassessed, particu-

The Western Pygmy-Blue is thought to be the world's smallest butterfly.

larly with the azures. The Spring Azure has now been split into a number of species. While the taxonomy is still unsettled, it is known today that the Summer Azure, which was once thought to be a midsummer second flight of the Spring Azure, is a separate species.

Various species of azures and blues can often be confused. Spotters will find that azures usually display stronger flight and fly higher above the ground, while some blues, such as the Eastern Tailed Blue, flutter low to the ground, often through vegetation, and can be easily overlooked by butterfly seekers. Blues perform hindwing rubbing. Look for good nectar sources and moist areas where blues concentrate. A common spring sight is of dozens or at times even hundreds of Spring Azures drinking from damp mud on woodland roads. In the West we've enjoyed puddle parties of hundreds of mixed blues.

The world's smallest butterfly is a blue, the

Western Pygmy-Blue. Some individuals have only a ⅜-inch wingspan. Amazingly, this tiny butterfly is thought to be partially migratory and stages regular irruptions. (In contrast, you might be interested to know that the world's *largest* butterfly is the Queen Alexandra's Birdwing, found in Papua, New Guinea, with a wingspan of up to 12 inches.)

Some blues are highly specific in their host plant preferences and in habitat needs. Because of this, some of North America's most endangered butterflies are blues. Karner Blue populations have been greatly impacted and reduced in New England and New York; the Mission Blue is nearly extinct in San Francisco. Both are victims of habitat loss to housing. The one butterfly known to have become extinct in North America is the Xerces Blue, formerly found in the San Francisco Bay area. Its name has been commemorated in the Xerces Society; the butterfly and the group today are synonymous with butterfly and insect conservation efforts.

The flight of most Lycaenids is fast, whirling, and erratic, unlike the more predictable and fairly direct flight of most other butterflies. This poses problems for the butterfly watcher, since they can disappear in a flash. Spotters soon learn, though, that Lycaenids may be refound through diligent searching, since after taking flight they frequently alight again within a few yards. Hairstreaks are the fastest, while coppers and blues are not quite as swift. Hairstreaks will nearly always perch with their wings closed, so that only the underside of the wing is visible. They are lateral baskers. Coppers and blues will rest with the wings closed, but bask in the sun with the wings open or partially open, giving watchers views of the upper wing surface. Observers are often confused when a flushed azure flashes brilliant blue, lands, and becomes a white butterfly with only the underside of the wings showing. The patient observer may get to see the brilliant blue again as the azure slowly opens its wings to warm up in the sun.

In the spring when nectar is scarce, searching for Lycaenids takes a keen eye since they often spend much of their day resting on leaves or on the ground in the vicinity of their host plant. Be alert for every flicker of movement, no matter how small the creature. Follow it with your eye, and when it lands bring it into focus with binoculars. You just may find yourself enjoying a jewel of a hairstreak, blue, or elfin. Tapping host plants gently may flush otherwise overlooked Lycaenids. When they land again be ready with your binoculars. In just this way we have found 'Olive' Juniper Hairstreaks where redcedar grows and Banded Hairstreaks by tapping young oak trees.

As summer unfolds and lush stands of wildflowers bloom, hairstreaks, coppers, and blues concentrate at rich nectar sources and become much easier to locate. Because of their tiny size, their stillness while nectaring, and their ability to camouflage well with flower buds, they are often overlooked. Keep this in mind and be sure to scan ahead when you spot good nectar sources. Study every flower head with your binoculars, and you will be rewarded with excellent looks at a variety of hairstreaks, coppers, and blues.

For target species learn timing, range, habitat, and host-plant needs. Then select sites within range and habitat where both host

The Malachite is a large southern brushfoot partial to rotting fruit.

plants and concentrations of favorite nectar sources occur. This sort of research pays off and is essential to finding some of the rarer or more localized Lycaenids. Each May in the New Jersey pine barrens we seek Hessel's Hairstreaks on blooming sand myrtle and highbush huckleberry near stands of their host plant, white-cedar. In Maryland, near woods with mistletoe, Great Purple Hairstreaks and other hairstreaks, coppers, and blues nectar on common milkweed and buttonbush in June, on Hercules' club in July and August, and on goldenrods in September. In Arizona in August we have enjoyed Great Purple Hairstreaks and a host of other Lycaenids on stands of blooming *Baccharis* along streams and seeps. We have had our only looks at Eastern Pygmy-Blues by frequenting marshy habitats within their range where *Salicornia* grows. In tropical pinelands on the Florida Keys we have enjoyed Bartram's Scrub-Hairstreaks nectaring on their host plant, woolly croton, where little else was in bloom. We make an annual pilgrimage in May to localized sites in the New Jersey pine barrens where bearberry flourishes, and at times we have studied dozens and dozens of Hoary Elfins nectaring on bearberry, their host plant.

Any blooming milkweed or *Eupatorium* should prompt the butterfly spotter to stop and study the flowers very closely. Along with the obvious big and showy butterflies, you should also find an assortment of nectaring Lycaenids. Certain garden plants, such as sedum, are Lycaenid magnets. Be sure to learn

of these for your area and save room for them in your garden plan.

BRUSH-FOOTED BUTTERFLIES
(NYMPHALIDAE)

Except for the Lycaenids, the Nymphalids are the largest and most diverse family of butterflies in the world. Many of our most familiar, showy, colorful, or eye-catching butterflies are Nymphalids. Both the milkweed butterflies (including the Monarch) and the satyrs are Nymphalids, but are often treated separately. This huge family, with about 4,500 species worldwide and approximately 200 occurring in North America north of Mexico, has confusing and even controversial taxonomy (systematics). Even expert lepidopterists cannot agree on what constitutes a "proper" Nymphalid or how the groups are related. Brushfoots are widespread and highly diverse, ranging in size from tiny crescents to huge, tailed daggerwings. They range in color from the green Malachite to orange-colored leafwings that can "disappear" before your eyes because they look so much like a dead leaf when perched. Many brushfoots are cryptically marked below, so that when perched with their wings closed they are very well camouflaged and difficult to locate.

Nymphalids are called brush-footed butterflies because their forelegs are very small and covered with bristlelike hairs, vaguely resembling a brush. All adult butterflies have three pairs of legs, but brushfoots walk on only the middle legs and hindlegs. The forelegs are usually less than half the normal size and contain important host plant sensors or detectors. With these, the butterflies "taste" their specific, required host plant. Also, the hindlegs in brushfoots can detect sugar when searching for nectar plants from which to drink.

The larvae of Nymphalids are particularly interesting. The later instars often have branching spines or "antlers," hairy ornaments that no doubt serve as predator deterrents. Being large and often boldly marked, they, along with swallowtail larvae, are the ones most often and easily spotted by butterfliers who enjoy specializing in searching for the caterpillar stage of the butterfly life cycle.

Brushfoots have a fairly rapid and direct flight. Some, such as the Red Admiral, are exasperatingly quick; others, such as fritillaries, are fairly easily followed. Many are very strong fliers; some are incredible migrants. The movements of Common Buckeyes, Red Admirals, and Painted Ladies nearly rival those of the Monarch, as they repopulate northern latitudes through migration and successive broods. The final brood migrates south in the autumn. Relatively common or familiar brushfoots include the fritillaries, crescents, checkerspots, anglewings, Mourning Cloak, tortoiseshells, American Lady, Painted Lady, Red Admiral,

This garish caterpillar will metamorphose into a stylish adult American Lady.

The tiny Elada Checkerspot, a brushfoot found in southern Arizona and south Texas.

Common Buckeye, White Peacock, Malachite, Red-spotted Purple, Viceroy, sisters, Ruddy Daggerwing, leafwings, emperors, satyrs, alpines, arctics, and milkweed butterflies. Red Admiral, Painted Lady, and American Lady, with huge ranges in North America south of the Arctic, are our most widespread, if not the most numerous, butterflies.

Emperors are medium-sized tawny and earth-colored brushfoots that use various hackberry trees as their host plant. Learn to identify hackberry trees if you hope to find Tawny Emperor, Hackberry Emperor, or Empress Leilia, since they are all very localized and never found far from hackberry trees. Emperors are strong fliers with a distinctive flap-flap-glide flight. They often treetop on their host plant. Emperors prefer tree sap and rotting fruit to flower nectar. They may nectar, but only rarely. Butterfly spotters can attract emperors by putting out rotten fruit or by seeking sap flows, but will be successful only if the host plant, hackberry, is nearby.

Anglewings, so named for their sharp-angled, sculptured wing borders, also rarely nectar and are therefore best found either puddling or at tree sap or fruit. The Question Mark, widespread throughout the East, and the various commas are each named for a unique silver marking on the underside of the hindwing; the mark looks like their name. We jokingly call an unidentified anglewing a "punctuation mark butterfly." The Question Mark is highly migratory, staging dramatic flights along the East Coast in both spring and fall. Look for them mainly in woodlands — try sunny glades in early spring. They are most active in early morning and late afternoon, and largely inactive on hot summer days.

The **checkerspots** and **crescents** number

about 42 species of small to medium-sized brushfoots which, as their name implies, generally show a bright, bold, checkered patterning, usually in blacks, golds, and oranges. To find checkerspots and crescents, find good nectar sources. Butterfly weed, daisy fleabane, and various knapweeds and goldenrods are excellent in the East. *Baccharis* thickets are great, in season, in the West. Although many checkerspots and crescents are single-brooded and localized near their host plants, they readily spread their wings as they nectar at flowers and therefore catch the eye. Many species of this group are particularly difficult to identify, especially in the West where they abound. Try to take a good photograph, so you can later compare it to field guides at your leisure and confirm your field identification.

Fritillaries are medium to large brushfoots, with 30 or so species found in the United States from the Mexican border to the Arctic. They are largely northern in distribution, usually found in forested areas or at high altitudes. In some parts of the country where many species of fritillaries are found, they can be tough to tell apart. Virtually all fritillaries use violets as their host plant and so are dependent on specialized habitats where violets flourish, such as fresh woodland openings. In the Arctic, some use other host plants, such as blueberry, crowberry, and mountain avens. Their flight is strong and on a straight line. All are cooperative baskers and nectarers, at least at some point during the day. Search for good nectar sources, watch, and wait; patrolling fritillaries will eventually drop by to drink. Stands of lantana, thistle, common milkweed, butterfly weed, bee balm, knapweed, and garden zinnias are good places to check. Some fritillaries (and some crescents) are sexually dimorphic. Almost all are stunning, favorite finds for the butterfly watcher.

The dramatic Great Spangled Fritillary is the East's most common fritillary.

SATYRS
(NYMPHALIDAE,
SUBFAMILY SATYRINAE)

Biologists today lump the **satyrs,** once considered a separate family (Satyridae), within the Brushfoot family. Nonetheless, their distinct patterns and behavior dictate that, for watchers at least, the satyrs will always be a separate grouping. More than 2,000 species of satyrs occur worldwide, with 45 found in North America north of the Mexican border. Most are medium-sized butterflies, with soft brown coloration, numerous eyespots, and cryptic patterning offering excellent camouflage. Because of this satyrs rarely catch the eye and must be sought out by butterfly spotters. Not only are they very well camouflaged, but their flight is slow, erratic, and low to the ground through grasses or sedges or just over the grass tops. Some species are specific to wet

---

Southern Pearly-Eyes, like other satyrs, are soft brown and cryptically patterned.

meadows, swamps, or slow-moving streams where sedges and grasses proliferate. Satyrs use grasses or sedges as host plants and are never found far from them. Butterfly spotters must target the proper habitat and season to find satyrs. Woodlands with openings where sunlight can reach the ground and encourage lush stands of grasses are perfect settings to look for satyrs, just as dark forests with little sunlight and few grasses are not. Male satyrs patrol along woodland trails and shady wooded edges. Their patrolling flight will inevitably route them back by a patient observer. Only a few of the satyrs nectar at flowers and then only infrequently, but all are attracted to rotting fruit, sap flows, and bird and animal droppings. Search for rotting fruit, such as persimmon, apple, or pear, particularly in shady areas. In yards and gardens try putting out a dish of watermelon slices or rotten bananas. With such an offering we regularly attract Common Wood-Nymph, Little Wood-Satyr, and Appalachian Brown to our yard.

Some satyrs are extremely common and widespread, such as the Little Wood-Satyr, a forest dweller common throughout the East, and the large Common Wood-Nymph, abundant throughout most of the United States during its one flight. The Common Ringlet is abundant in prairie habitat in the West and North. Other satyrs can be rare; the Mitchell's Satyr is listed as endangered. Found today largely only in Michigan, it was extirpated from northern New Jersey bogs by relentless pressure from unscrupulous collectors.

Alpines and **arctics** are northern and high-altitude satyrs. Found in alpine meadows, treeline forest, and Arctic tundra, most are covered

How to Spot Butterflies

with dense, bristly "hairs," which help insulate them against heat loss. Most are dark, to better absorb heat in chilly conditions, and are particularly cryptically colored. They bask with closed wings deep in tundra grasses and lichens, almost impossible to spot unless you see exactly where they land. Remarkably, some species are biennial, the adults flying only every other year since it takes two years for the insect to complete its life cycle in the short, cold Arctic summers. Alpines and arctics are exciting finds for the butterflier. When you're in their special habitat, look for them nectaring low on the tundra, on flowers such as mountain avens and Lapland rosebay, though your best bet is to flush them as you hike. Upon being flushed, they may fly long distances before realighting, and they have led us on some great games of alpine hide-and-seek in spectacular wilderness areas high above treeline.

THE MONARCH AND OTHER MILKWEED BUTTERFLIES
(NYMPHALIDAE, SUBFAMILY DANAINAE)

The Monarch and its close relatives, the Queen and the Soldier, are in the subfamily Danainae and are known as the "milkweed butterflies." Most authorities consider them a subfamily of the brushfoots. There are about 200 species of milkweed butterflies, widespread in the tropical and subtropical regions of the planet. They all use plants in the milkweed family as their larval foodplant.

In the southern United States three milkweed butterflies are found: Monarch, Queen, and Soldier. The Monarch is the only milkweed butterfly that occurs in the northern United States, and they are found as far north as southern Canada. Of the 108 species of milkweed found in North America, Monarchs are known to lay eggs on at least 27 species. Monarch population density varies across their range depending on the distribution of these milkweed species.

For many years, we have thought of the Monarch as "our" butterfly, a North American species that migrates to the tropics in winter, but evolutionarily it is the other way around. Monarchs developed in the tropics and over millions of generations evolved their migratory habit of moving north in spring to take advantage of vast untapped milkweed resources.

Because milkweed butterflies lay their eggs on various species of milkweed, most of which are toxic, their caterpillars, and eventually adult milkweed butterflies, are unpalatable to most birds. This protection from predators has, in turn, led to well-known and well-studied mimicry. It was long believed that the Viceroy mimicked the Monarch, but it has recently been learned that the Viceroy probably is as unpalatable as the Monarch and, therefore, not an example of true mimicry, though each no doubt benefits from looking like the other — a predator need eat only one of either species to learn to avoid both.

While many other butterflies flit quickly and dash about to avoid being caught by predators, milkweed butterflies sail and glide along slowly. This is probably a result of their

The Queen is a milkweed butterfly of the Deep South, occasionally straying north.

being poisonous and not needing the quick, evasive flight of most butterflies. Butterfly spotters may narrow down an identification by noticing this distinctive manner of flight.

Monarchs are strong fliers, however. In their remarkable migrations, they can fly up to 20 miles an hour and have been recorded at heights of more than 10,000 feet. They are such strong fliers that over time they have even colonized Australia, New Zealand, and the Canary Islands. They are a regular vagrant to Britain.

The male of each of our milkweed butterflies can be told from the female by a conspicuous black spot on a vein in each hindwing, often called a scent patch. The female has no scent patch; she has thicker black scaling along the wing veins, making her veins appear to be wider and darker.

The Queen is a resident of south Florida, south Texas, and southern California, but sometimes performs major movements, form-

ing temporary colonies as far north as Colorado. The Soldier is more sedentary and less common, a resident in south Florida, and seasonal in south Texas and Arizona from August to January.

In the early spring Monarchs are scarce and do not linger. They are on the move, searching for milkweed plants just breaking through the ground, and will lay their eggs on 1-inch-tall plant tips. Some springs a few individuals are seen before milkweed has broken ground, and butterfly spotters cannot help but wonder what their fate will be. By early summer, when wildflowers begin to flourish on road shoulders and in fallow fields, Monarchs are easier to find, especially by targeting good nectar sources.

All milkweed butterflies nectar and are regular visitors to butterfly gardens. By simply incorporating a variety of native milkweeds into your garden plan you will almost guarantee that milkweed butterflies will linger to mate and lay eggs, filling your garden through the summer with generation after generation of Monarchs and, in the Deep South, Queens and Soldiers. Similarly, a plot of milkweed in the wild will inevitably draw in milkweed butterflies. To find milkweed butterflies while afield, search for good nectar sources such as the various milkweeds, thistles, verbenas, bee balms, asters, goldenrods, sunflowers, *Eupatoriums*, ironweed, lantana, and stands of *Baccharis*.

THE MONARCH

In 1975, when scientists discovered where Monarchs go each fall from throughout the East, Pat had recently moved to Cape May. Clay grew up in South Jersey and was very familiar with the massing of Monarchs after au-

How to Spot Butterflies

tumn cold fronts, when one could find them roosting by the hundreds — and some evenings by the thousands — in densely vegetated beachfront stretches, but to Pat it was a rich new experience, one more incredible natural history wonder to marvel at, and one that captivates her to this day.

National Geographic's August 1976 issue first shared with the world leading Monarch researcher Fred Urquhart's discovery, the incredible story of the Monarch, how all eastern Monarchs — those throughout southern Canada and the United States east of the Rocky Mountains (involving millions upon millions of individuals) — migrate each fall, August through early December, to reach high, fir forest–covered mountains in central Mexico, where they overwinter until the following spring. Accompanying the article were hard-to-believe photographs of tree trunks and weighted-down branches hidden under layer upon layer of Monarchs.

Twenty years after the world learned of this amazing discovery, we were fortunate to journey there ourselves. We left a snowy, bone-chilling cold New Jersey behind in mid-January and accompanied Jeffrey Glassberg on one of his Butterflies Through Binoculars Tours to the high mountains in Mexico where all eastern Monarchs spend the winter. We had just read a recently published in-depth article on Monarchs by Lincoln Brower, noted Monarch researcher, and were brimming over with new understanding and excitement.

It was a naturalist's dream vacation. We've led butterfly walks at Cape May for 20 years while Monarchs migrated through by the thousands, yet struggled to answer questions about their migration and destination. Do they sleep through the winter? Are they dormant as they cling to the mountaintop fir trees? Do they fly and nectar in winter? So much of our knowledge was based on information gleaned from articles published by the scientific community and even from children's books. The little that was in print offered conflicting information, so we could hardly wait to experience it firsthand.

We traveled to the tiny town of Angangueo, about 100 miles west of Mexico City. Though a relatively short distance, the journey took most of the day as we went higher and higher into the mountains. Angangueo lies on a valley floor high in the mountains (at about 8,000 feet elevation) with mountains rising up on either side of the charming town. Pastel-colored houses line the main street. Pride in the nearby Monarch roost is obvious, and many of the hotels had signs welcoming Monarchs and Monarch watchers.

The next morning we traveled one hour farther up into the mountains on narrow, switchback roads in the back of a pickup truck. Along the way, clear-cut mountainsides were terraced for farming on unbelievably steep slopes. It was hard to imagine anyone harvesting crops on such steep hillsides.

By 1986 ten significant Monarch overwintering sites were known in Mexico. They are all within a small area of about 480 square miles in the center of a 30- to 60-mile-wide belt of volcanic mountains and valleys that stretches 500 miles across Mexico. The overwintering sites are on nine separate mountain peaks, all between 40 and 100 miles west of Mexico City in the states of Mexico and Michoacan. About 100 million Monarchs spend the winter there, arriving in November and remaining until the middle of March. Some of the overwintering colonies take up the size of a baseball diamond, others are as large as a city block, but all occur where stands of Oyamel fir trees grow. These fir trees are specialized for high-altitude areas, a type of boreal forest not unlike those found in northern Canada.

Our visit was to *El Rosario,* the Rosario Butterfly Sanctuary in the Sierra Campanario. In 1996 a second site opened to the public — the Chincua Butterfly Sanctuary in the Sierra Chincua. These two sites are the most accessible to the general public. The route up to the gates at *El Rosario* was lined with stalls selling an assortment of food, beverages, linens, crafts, and other souvenirs, all with Monarch motifs. Even though it was midweek, many Mexicans were also there to see the Monarch roost. A nominal fee amounting to several dollars was collected and the re-

quired guide assigned to us. We hired an additional guide to help carry our cameras and tripods and were pleased to pay for their services and to help the local economy through this ecotourism arrangement.

Tremendous effort has gone into setting up this roost for visitors. Steps, set into the steep mountain paths, keep erosion from occurring. Many stretches also have railings to ease the long climb. Benches scattered along the trail are a welcome sight. We eventually climbed to about 10,000 feet elevation. We flatlanders were pretty winded and even more grateful for the hired guides, who carried our heavy load of optics. Twenty Mexican schoolchildren passed us on the way up to the roost, and, before we'd even reached the site, they passed us again on their way down. An 80-year-old Mexican woman reached the roost as we did. The look on her face was not one of exhaustion, as we half-expected, but one of total wonder!

A BLIZZARD OF BUTTERFLIES

The Monarchs move around within the roost through the winter. When they first arrive in November they form dispersed colonies on or near ridgelines at the highest elevations. By December and January they form concentrated roosts in forests on the steepest slopes. As temperatures warm in February and March they move to concentrated roosts at even lower elevations. On our visit in mid-January they were about a two-hour hike up the mountain.

Just before reaching the roost site, the forest mountain trail led out onto an open meadow. We found thousands of Monarchs puddling in a wet seep that trickled across the meadow. They were drinking water, something none of us had ever seen Monarchs do back home. Others poured out of the fir forest and across the meadow by the thousands. Though mesmerized by the scene, we continued along the trail, which took us back into the fir forest and to the roost itself.

At the heart of the roost the dark Oyamel fir trees were darker yet because of their covering — huge honeycombs of Monarchs. Millions upon millions of perched Monarchs weighed down branches and covered trunks. Flying Monarchs poured through the trees, filling the sky overhead, and floated toward us down the trail. It looked like orange confetti was being sprinkled through the forest.

We stood in a river of Monarchs, unable to move, transfixed by the wonder of it. We'd feel soft taps as they would briefly land on us — on a shoulder, in our hair, on our backs. The sound of millions of Monarchs on the wing was bewitching. Jane Scott, Jeff Glassberg's wife, thought it sounded like breezes through palm tree branches on a beach. The whisper of wings was a constant companion, a butterfly breeze.

Jane Ruffin, who has ardently tagged migrating Monarchs in New Jersey and Pennsylvania for years, scanned and scanned through her telescope up into the Monarch-covered trees, hoping to spot a tagged butterfly. It was far harder than finding a needle in a haystack, and, unfortunately, she was unsuccessful. Over the years, many Monarchs

tagged in the United States have been found at the roost.

Even though we saw millions of Monarchs float by us as the sun warmed branches in their inner roost, the roost trees looked no different, no less covered, with every branch and trunk still layered and heavy with Monarchs. By 3:00 P.M., when the sun began to drop and the temperature with it, it was as if a switch was thrown and the Monarchs reversed their course, floating back up the mountain to set-

About 100 million Monarchs winter in mountaintop Oyamel fir trees in Mexico.

tle again on the already heavily laden branches at the roost.

The following day, anxious to learn how early in the morning Monarchs left the roost, Jane Ruffin and Pat hoofed it up the mountain in a mere 45 minutes and arrived at the inner roost by about 10:00 A.M. A couple from New Zealand was already there and reported that when they arrived at 9:00 A.M. the Monarchs were "still sleeping." The beginning of their activity was around 10:15 A.M., and the first ones floated down through the dark forest where shafts of light filtered through, like the first big flakes of an impending snowstorm. As the sun rose farther and lit Monarch-festooned branches and tree trunks, sheets of them peeled away in a flutter of flight, a waterfall of Monarchs through the forest. Again the trees looked no different, with masses of Monarchs remaining.

Farther down the mountain Bill Ruffin and Clay watched as a flock of 20 Black-backed Orioles flitted out from branches and caught Monarchs in flight, as a flycatcher might, and then returned to their perch to feed on them. Monarch wings floated down from the perches, spinning in the air like winged maple seeds. Along with the orioles, wintering Black-headed Grosbeaks have learned to feed on Monarchs in the roost, and Black-eared Mice prey on Monarchs that land on the forest floor. Scientists estimate that as many as one million Monarchs are consumed by these three major predators over the course of a winter. Winter storms can take a toll as well. An estimated five million Monarchs were killed in a December 1995 storm.

Later that afternoon we found Monarchs the entire way down the mountain and even along the road back to Angangueo. Many were at wet spots on the ground, but others were nectaring on a white bushlike *Eupatorium* and on a yellow bushlike *Senecio*. This was all rich information for a group of keen naturalists, to learn that Monarchs not only fly extensively at their winter roost, but puddle and nectar as well.

These Mexican high-mountain roosts offer a delicate balance of conditions to the overwintering Monarchs. Temperatures are usually close to but not quite freezing, keeping the butterflies sluggish so they do not use up their energy reserves, but not cold enough to kill them. The dense, towering Oyamel fir trees offer protection from snow and rain to clusters of roosting Monarchs. The southwest-facing slopes, where roosts are found, receive good amounts of moisture from fog and clouds, keeping the Monarchs moist so they don't dry out from the wind and cold, but not so wet and cold that they freeze and die.

Logging remains a major threat to the roosts. Trees cut on the edges of and in mountain roosts allow cold winds, rain, snow, and hail into the heart of the roost and break down the delicate balance of conditions — temperature, humidity, and sunlight. While we were in Angangueo, trucks loaded with huge freshly cut trees rolled by, one after another. A decree issued by the president of Mexico in 1986 protects five major overwintering sites (of the nine then known) by setting them aside as designated sanctuaries totaling 62 square miles. Logging continues in unprotected buffer areas around all of the colonies, and, in some cases, illegally within the roosts. The wood is being harvested for home building, heating, and cooking. Some of the people who need new homes are the very people drawn to the area in hopes of finding jobs related to the tourists visiting the roost sites. Some of the hotels housing ecotourists visiting the roosts heat their rooms with fireplaces. Efforts begun in 1993 for a town-sponsored tree nursery at *El Rosario* met with some success. About 261 families became involved, and 130,500 Oyamel fir trees were planted. They were 3 feet tall three years later when we visited, nearly ready to be moved to the high slopes. Each group that visits the overwintering colonies in Mexico benefits and strengthens the area's economy, helping to convince the local residents and landowners not to cut the very trees responsible for this flood of visitors. Our visit to the overwintering sites in Mexico was with Jeffrey Glassberg's Butterflies Through Binoculars Tours. Monarch researcher Dr. William Calvert also offers tours, as does Victor Emanuel Nature Tours (VENT). (See Further Information.)

As winter nears an end and the days grow longer, the Monarchs become more active and begin to mate. At the end of the mating frenzy they begin their journey north, leaving the roost around the second week of March. Once they've mated they have only a month or so longer to live. Females, now full of fertile eggs, fly north and east, laying eggs on milkweed as they go, getting perhaps as far north as the Gulf states before they die. Their eggs hatch into tiny caterpillars. The caterpillars feed ravenously on milkweed buds and leaves and grow to full size, pupate, and emerge as adults ("children" of the overwintering population). These Monarchs journey farther north, mating as they go and laying their eggs along the way. These eggs mature into the "grandchildren" of the overwintering population. So it goes, until Monarchs repopulate all of the United States and the southern edge of Canada.

MONARCHS IN THE UNITED STATES AND CANADA

Northbound Monarchs are first seen around Baton Rouge, Louisiana, by mid-March. We first see them in southern New Jersey between April 7 and April 23. Milkweed is just peeking through the ground by about April 23 in southern New Jersey — all they need for egg laying to occur. Monarchs leapfrog north, generation after generation slowly repopulating the eastern half of North America, reaching Canada last because it is farthest away.

Throughout the summer, generation after generation of Monarch butterflies entertain us. Each individual adult Monarch butterfly lives only about two to five weeks. Monarchs mate and create the next generation by laying eggs on milkweed plants, often on the underside of a leaf or on the flower buds. The egg is minute and can be easily overlooked. The tiny caterpillar hatches from the egg and becomes an eating machine. It takes the caterpillar 9 to 14 days of almost nonstop eating until it is full-size, about 2¾ inches. When the caterpillar is full-size it attaches itself to a safe spot, either on the very plant it has been eating or sometimes some distance away, and goes into a J position. It hangs in this position for about 24 hours, still looking like a caterpillar. Then, the caterpillar goes through

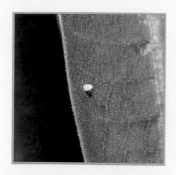  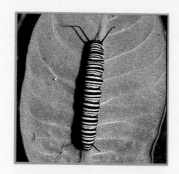

The Monarch Life Cycle

(begin with photo at top left and work clockwise)

Day 1: egg laid on common milkweed; **Day 4:** caterpillar hatches; **Day 16:** caterpillar nearly full size — notice tiny newly laid Monarch egg to left of caterpillar; **Day 17:** caterpillar goes into a J position and hangs there for 24 hours; **Day 18:** caterpillar molts final time and transforms into the chrysalis in just minutes; **Days 18–27:** the chrysalis, a green jewel, hangs suspended; **Day 28** (4 photos): the chrysalis becomes transparent and the Monarch is visible through it. It takes just 80 seconds for the butterfly to emerge. It pumps fluids into its rumpled wings, and several hours later it is dry and ready to take flight.

a final molt and transforms into the chrysalis in just four minutes, a transformation easily missed unless you are glued to the spot. The chrysalis, a green jewel, hangs suspended for 8 to 11 days. It appears to become transparent toward the end of this period, and you can see the Monarch's wings and body parts through it, as scales and coloration develop. It takes the adult butterfly about 80 seconds to emerge, so you can easily miss this event, too, unless you are on constant vigil. Once emerged, the adult butterfly slowly pumps fluids into its rumpled wings. After several hours it is ready to take flight and begin its life stage as an adult winged butterfly. In the Mid-Atlantic states, from egg to adult butterfly may take only 20 days in July, but up to 36 or more days later in the fall when it gets cooler.

The freshly emerged Monarchs are able to mate when they are three to eight days old. Mating takes some time, often from one afternoon until the following morning. Females begin laying eggs right after their first mating. Eggs are laid singly on milkweed. During their three- to five-week lifespan, both the male and the female will mate several times. Females lay about 700 eggs over a two- to five-week period.

In the fall, as daylight decreases, a chemical reaction in the caterpillar triggers it to develop into a sexually immature butterfly, a butterfly that migrates south instead of mating. Caterpillars can tell the difference between 12 and 14 hours of daylight. The final fall generation of Monarchs leaves Canada earliest because day length shortens earlier in the North. Migration is often noted by mid-August. Farther south in New Jersey, Monarchs might still be found mating and laying eggs into September and October, creating the final fall generation for the Mid-Atlantic region much later.

A MIRACULOUS MIGRATION

The Monarch's lengthy two-way migration is unique among butterflies throughout the world. Scientists estimate that there are up to 100 million Monarchs by the fall of each year, though these numbers can vary greatly from year to year. Lincoln Brower, a leading Monarch researcher, theorizes that years with huge numbers during the fall migration directly relate to two factors: 1) mild conditions at the winter roost in Mexico the previous winter, and 2) warm and clear weather, along with adequate rainfall for favorable growing conditions for milkweeds and nectar sources, spring through summer, throughout their summer range in the United States and Canada. Conversely, years of small numbers during fall migration follow stormy winters at the winter roost and overcast, wet, and cold weather spring through summer (or an exceptionally dry summer) in their northern summer range.

There are two different populations of Monarchs. The so-called eastern population is large and found from the Rocky Mountains east to the Atlantic Ocean and north to southern Canada. It is the eastern population's final fall generation that migrates south to the overwintering sites in Mexico, some traveling more than 2,000 miles. The western population is much smaller. Scientists believe that there are about five million butterflies in the western population. They are found west of the Rocky Mountains to the Pacific Ocean and north to southern Canada. The western population's final fall generation migrates only several hundred miles to coastal California to 150 major winter roost sites (and 100 or so lesser sites), most of which are within two miles of the coast between just north of San Francisco and northern Baja California in Mexico, where they congregate from October through March. Each of the major sites harbors 10,000–40,000 Monarchs, and some years many more; the lesser sites attract small numbers of Monarchs, 100 or fewer. In coastal California, roosting Monarchs cover stands of eucalyptus trees, Monterey pines, and Monterey cypresses. Many of the overwintering sites in California are severely threatened by coastal development pressures. The Monarch Project, created by conservationists in 1984, works to preserve California overwintering sites through conservation easements, zoning laws, land-use plans, and purchase. An astounding $2 million bond was passed by Californians in 1988 to purchase Monarch sites. Some sites in California have celebrated and protected their wintering Monarchs since the 1930s; the city of Pacific Grove passed an ordinance in 1939 authorizing a $1,000 fine for "molesting a butterfly in any way."

It is important to know, however, that recent landmark research by Robert Michael Pyle has determined that many "western" Monarchs indeed do not go to the Pacific Coast as previously assumed, but migrate through and around the Rocky Mountains — going to the Mexican mountaintop roosts as do their eastern counterparts. These wonderful observational studies are causing us to rethink our suppositions regarding the western populations and underscore the complexities of Monarch conservation.

Each fall millions of Monarchs migrate south, emptying out the entire United States and southern Canada. These migrants, composed of the final fall generation, are focused on migration rather than mating, so they are said to be in "reproductive diapause." They will not mate or lay eggs until the following spring; this generation will therefore live eight or nine months as adults. A brief summer season in Canada and the northern United States results in fewer generations (about three), and from these northern areas the final fall generation of Monarchs begins to migrate as early as August and early September. Farther south, where the summer season is longer, more generations occur (four to five), and the final fall generation does not migrate until late September, October, and even through November and early December. Therefore, northern Monarchs are migrating while more southerly populations are still mating, laying eggs, and dying. Fluctuating numbers of Monarchs try to overwinter in a few sites north of central Mexico, in Florida, and other states along the Gulf Coast. Some winters they survive, but most winters they are killed by frost.

Monarch migration is a spectacle. Mid-September through October at Cape May, lush stands of seaside goldenrod in the dunes are weighted with them. Butterfly bushes and patches of sedum and New England asters in backyard gardens can be covered. Nectaring as they go, Monarchs actually gain weight while migrating. Evening roosts in protected spots, on the leeward side of trees and shrubs, attract hundreds and some nights thousands of

Monarchs. At rest they all close their wings and almost disappear, easily mistaken for dead leaves. When a newcomer flutters by, they all open their wings as if to welcome it and let it know of their safe haven. Once the newcomer has settled into the roost they all close their wings once again.

Fred Urquhart involved 3,000 volunteers in a tagging project between 1952 and 1976. In recent years Monarch Watch has brought together thousands of students and adults in tagging efforts. Participants involved in Monarch Watch (see Further Information) tagged 50,000 Monarchs in 1997 alone. Through years of tagging, wonderful facts about Monarch migration have been fine-tuned. Researchers have learned that Monarchs fly an average of 1,800 miles, with flights of more than 3,000 miles documented. They can cover up to 86 miles in a day and take about two months to reach their overwintering sites in Mexico. Winds and landforms concentrate them, just as these same conditions concentrate other migrants (birds, bats, and dragonflies). They instinctively seek tail winds when traveling. It is completely unknown how they navigate or how they locate the Mexican mountain winter roosts. Who would disagree that Monarch migration is a true miracle of nature?

SKIPPERS
(HESPERIIDAE)

Skippers are medium to small fast-moving butterflies, so named for their rapid, streaking, bobbing flight. They appear to skip over veg-etation, putting down momentarily only to take off again. They can be the hardest butterflies to watch, perplexing in their ability to seemingly vanish before your eyes. Indeed, take-offs and flight can be so rapid that, at times, you have no clue which way they went!

Many older butterfly books omitted skippers, partially because they were relatively unstudied or poorly understood, but also because some taxonomists considered them to be closely related but separate from butterflies. They are, in fact, a relatively primitive butterfly, with some similarities to moths. Skippers are distinct in having the antennae clubs bent.

There are an estimated 3,700 species of skippers worldwide. Luckily for the identification-challenged, there are "only" about 270 in the United States and Canada! Skippers are the largest and most diverse family of butterflies in North America. Many are "little brown jobs" (LBJs) and can tax the identification skills of even veteran butterfly watchers and lepidopterists. For those with a birding background, we can tell you that skippers make confusing fall warblers look easy, and identifying the "witches" (a complex of small, drab, brown, look-alike skipper species) is akin to identifying empidonax flycatchers, but without the aid of a song or call! Indeed, some skipper species can be identified positively only in the hand and a few only through collection and dissection! For these, we suggest the butterfly watcher "skip" them.

There are three main skipper groups. The **giant-skippers** are a complex group of about 13 tropical species ranging from the southern United States to Central America. They are aptly named — large, and usually distinctly marked. Uniquely, their larvae bore into fleshy leaves. The Yucca Giant-Skipper is the one most commonly encountered, ranging from the Carolinas south and west to California. Within range, search for the giant-skippers near their agave, manfreda, and yucca host plants.

Spread-winged skippers, found throughout our continent, are medium-sized skippers, including longtails, cloudywings, duskywings, and sootywings. These skippers bask and nectar with their wings open or spread. Some, such as the Mangrove Skipper, are quite spectacular. Many are difficult to identify, but they all usually give the observer a good look. Males patrol while looking for mates, often returning to the same exposed perch — a boon for watchers with binoculars and cameras. Their flight is swift, but they rarely go far when flushed. Some spread-wings, particularly some duskywings, are often tough to

A few skippers such as the Mangrove Skipper, are large and showy.

identify since they are all variations on the same theme. Others, such as the Long-tailed Skipper, are an easy identification. Late-fall wanderings of Long-tailed Skipper add spice to butterfly watching when individuals are found far north of their normal range. The Silver-spotted Skipper is distinctively patterned and bright and a staple throughout much of the United States, with many flights. In New Jersey, it is present in varying numbers from mid-April through mid-October. Active all day long from early morning to late in the day, even on cloudy days, it is feisty and aggressive, chasing other butterflies and even swooping on people and pets (what *are* they thinking?).

Grass skippers are so named because they all rely on various grasses or sedges as larval hosts. They are sometimes referred to as "branded skippers" because of the male's black stigma — a dark scent-producing patch, appearing like a brand on the upperside of the forewing. They are also variously called "folded-winged skippers," which refers to their habit of basking with their forewings open to about a 45° angle, with the hindwing open flat (a combination of both dorsal and lateral basking), an arrangement often confusing to watchers. They will also perch with their wings closed, with only the bottom surfaces showing as they hold them above their back. For some species, identification depends on seeing both the underside (perched) and upperside (basking), often very difficult under field conditions. Predominant colors are browns and oranges. Some are sexually dimorphic; there are many look-alike species, and some variations within species. Together these traits usually require a very good look (and even a good photograph) for positive identification. More so than any other butterfly group, wing wear can bring about changing patterns on skippers, and a worn individual may show a very different pattern from a fresh one.

Some grass skippers, such as the Dun Skipper, are widespread. Others, such as the Arogos Skipper and Reversed Roadside-Skipper, are highly localized and rare. Some, such as the Cobweb Skipper, have only one brief early spring flight period. Some, such as the Fiery Skipper, are true emigrants, straying far to the north during summer. The tiny European Skipper, introduced into the United States in 1910, has spread throughout the Northeast and Mid-Atlantic states.

In spring and early summer most skippers can be especially tough to see until there is nectar to concentrate them. This is true of butterfly watching in general in spring and during drought periods of sparse nectar. Choose suitable habitat where target species are likely and their host plants occur, and walk along slowly. Most skippers are small, nondescript, and blend in perfectly with their surroundings. Many perch on the ground or on leaves and branches. When flushed many dash off in a whirling, zigzag, hard-to-follow flight, but will land again sometimes right back at their original perch site. Be ready for any flicker of movement, and be prepared to follow their erratic flight. When they land use your binoculars to get a better look.

Once wildflowers abound in summer, skippers become easier to locate on good nectar sources. We have had some of our best luck finding skippers by seeking patches of blooming thistle, vetch, rattlebox, everlasting pea and other members of the Pea family, daisy fleabane, *Helenium*, knapweed, goldenrod, sunflowers, camphorweed, aster, *Bidens*, *Pluchea*, mints, pickerelweed, alligator weed, swamp and common milkweeds, dogbane, *Eupatorium*, bee balm, buttonbush, lippia, blue vervain, saltmarsh aster, sea ox-eye, sea lavender, and gardens with zinnias, butterfly bush, lantana, and sedum.

Skippers are a challenge, the hardest in all butterfly watching. Even after years of butterfly watching, when we visit new areas, we often leave the grass skippers for last. It can be hard to look at an LBJ in the grass as a California Sister floats past! Nonetheless, we always get back to them, for sorting out the skippers is one of the most satisfying of butterfly challenges to conquer.

OTHER BUTTERFLIES

There are a few other butterflies that do not readily fit the divisions or families outlined above. The **metalmarks** are a highly diverse group, found mainly in the Neotropics. They exhibit tremendous variation in size, color, and wing shape. Many are localized and uncommon. Twenty-three species are found in North America north of Mexico, mostly in the southern United States. Only three are found in the East: Northern Metalmark, Little Metalmark, and Swamp Metalmark. The eastern metalmarks are all small, orange-colored, and show metallic-looking silver flecking on the wings. They fly swiftly and erratically. Metalmarks can be quite elusive because of their habit of perching for lengthy periods of time on leaves on or near their host plant. In the West, Mormon Metalmark is large and widely distributed, while many others have very limited ranges. While seeking Lycaenids in the West on attractive nectar sources, you are also likely to find nectaring metalmarks, such as Palmer's, Fatal, Zela, and Ares Metalmarks. Some scientists believe metalmarks to be a subfamily of Lycaenidae, while others place them in their own family, the Riodiniadae, which is generally accepted today.

The **Harvester** is an unusual Lycaenid. Related to hairstreaks, it is found throughout the eastern United States. The Harvester has the distinction of being the only carnivorous butterfly in North America. This is because of the caterpillar's predacious habits; it feeds exclusively on aphids, usually the Woolly Aphid. Harvesters lay eggs among aphids. The eggs hatch, and the caterpillars begin to consume the aphids. Adult Harvesters never nectar, but drink aphid honeydew (secretions) and tree sap and feed on dung and carrion. They also puddle. Their flight is fast and erratic, a whirligig or whirling dervish–type flight, yet they rarely go far when flushed. They are a low-density species, never abundant. To find Harvesters, look for Woolly Aphids on alder, beech, and sometimes on other trees and shrubs. The butterfly will never be found away from aphid infestations. You can find signs of Harvesters in winter, by searching winter woods for distinctive aphid damage.

The **snouts**, once thought to be part of a separate family, are now considered to be a

The American Snout is named for its curious elongated palps.

type of Nymphalid. There are eight species worldwide, but only one in North America, the American Snout. This butterfly's name is derived from the curious elongated labial palps that extend in front of the face and eyes. This "snout" is thought to contribute to the butterfly's camouflage. When perched with its wings closed, the butterfly can look much like a leaf, the snout appearing to be the stem of the leaf.

American Snouts lay their eggs exclusively on various hackberry trees. They are uncommon in the Northeast, except where hackberry trees grow, and there they can be locally com-

Leafwings, such as this Tropical Leafwing, are difficult to spot when perched.

mon. Learning to recognize hackberry trees will determine your success in finding this butterfly. At times they are tremendously abundant in the Southwest. They are strong, swift fliers and they perform remarkable emigrations. During periodic population explosions millions can be seen in Texas and the lower Great Plains. Adult American Snouts nectar only rarely.

The **leafwings**, also known as goatweed butterflies, are another unusual brushfoot type. This tropical group includes six species found in the United States. Most occur in the South. The leafwing moniker refers to their remarkable camouflage. Most are bright orange above, but this is seen only in flight; they perch on tree trunks with the wings closed and uncannily resemble dead leaves. Some tropical leafwings are extraordinary in their resemblance of specific types of dead leaves. The Pale-spotted Leafwing is black and blue on top, but is also cryptically patterned below. Leafwings feed on rotting fruit, sap, and animal droppings, but never nectar at flowers. Look for them near fruit trees, or consider putting out a dish of rotting fruit. We have seen them sipping from a discarded banana peel. Our first Tropical Leafwing was enjoyed in an Arizona garden as it sipped from a dish of overripe, gooey mangoes. Leafwings are sometimes found in cool, shady areas near streams.

Leafwings are extremely difficult to spot when they are perched. Look for flying individuals and attempt to follow them with your eyes or your binoculars until they perch. Then creep close for a good look. While bicycling in Florida, we have flushed trailside Florida Leafwings, then watched them until they perched again. Then a slow approach allowed for study and photographs.

Heliconians are medium-sized, brilliantly patterned tropical brushfoots. More than 65 species are found in the American tropics, mainly associated with the rain forest, but only three species are common in the southern United States, with another four occurring as strays or vagrants. They are also known as the "longwings" because of their unique long-winged shape. Even though they are a type of Nymphalid, they differ in several ways morphologically. Adult heliconians are the only butterflies known to feed on pollen. They are also attracted to rich nectar sources. Their caterpillars feed on passionflower plants. These host plants are poisonous to birds, giving both the larvae and butterfly immunity to winged predators. Because of this, many other

Heliconians, tropical brushfoots, are also known as longwings. The Zebra *(left)* **and the Julia** *(right)* **are both found in Florida and Texas, sometimes emigrating north.**

tropical butterfly species mimic the heliconians in color and pattern to protect themselves. Some longwings have the unusual habit of forming communal roosts. Heliconians may be the most intelligent of all butterflies. Recent research has shown that they can learn flower colors, hence nectar availability, as fast as honey bees, which are usually thought to be among the most intelligent insects.

In the United States, Zebras and Julias are found in Florida and Texas, sometimes emigrating far to the north. The Gulf Fritillary (not a true fritillary) is the third common heliconian, a spectacular brilliant orange butterfly, patterned with silver below. Normally found year-round only in south Florida, south Texas, and southern California, they sometimes migrate far to the north, at times even reaching Canada. When one showed up in a garden at Cape May Point in September, despite a good hawk migration, its arrival emptied the famous hawkwatch platform as

naturalists flocked to see it. This Gulf Fritillary was only the second modern record for New Jersey and was enjoyed by at least one hundred butterfly enthusiasts as it nectared for several hours in a seaside backyard butterfly garden.

Finally, **parnassians** are found at the other end of North America, in the high-altitude mountains of the western United States and Canada. Parnassians, sometimes called apollos, are a type of Papilionid — related to the swallowtails. They differ considerably, however. Medium to large, they have no tails. The Phoebus Parnassian is widespread in the West; Clodius Parnassian is more restricted. Both look like large whites with black (and red) patterning. The Eversmann's Parnassian is yellow and is an Arctic species. The Phoebus Parnassian, adapted to chilly alpine and tundra habitats, flies at colder temperatures than any other butterfly. It has sometimes even been seen on the wing in snowstorms!

How to Spot Butterflies

Further Information

BUTTERFLY WATCHING

Brewer, Jo, and Dave Winter. 1986. *Butterflies and Moths, A Companion to Your Field Guide*. New York: Prentice-Hall, Inc. An excellent book.

Douglas, Matthew M. 1986. *The Lives of Butterflies*. Ann Arbor: The University of Michigan Press. Excellent presentation of advanced information on the biology of butterflies.

Eyewitness Books. 1988. *Butterfly & Moth*. New York: Alfred A. Knopf, Inc. Illustrated with beautiful photos of live butterflies, moths, caterpillars, and life cycle, along with color photos of museum specimens. Very graphic way of conveying complicated information; children's book, but helpful for adult audience too.

Feltwell, John. 1986. *The Natural History of Butterflies*. New York: Facts On File. This book is rich in natural history information; a must for your library! The species discussed are those of Europe and North Africa, but the information about them can be easily applied to butterflies anywhere. Written in a highly readable fashion; essays cover how butterflies live, how and why they have such wonderful colors, how they court, interact with wild plants, react to sunshine and cloud cover, migrate, choose habitats, defend territories, and build populations.

Glassberg, Jeffrey. 1995. *Enjoying Butterflies More*. Marietta, Ohio: Bird Watcher's Digest. A wonderful booklet for the butterfly enthusiast. Covers butterfly biology, anatomy, where and when to look for butterflies, behavior, attracting (gardening for), identification, photography, conservation, and butterfly clubs.

Klass, Carolyn, and Robert Dirig. 1992. *Learning About Butterflies* (4-H Member/Leader Guide 139-M-9). Ithaca, New York: Cornell Cooperative Extension/Cornell University. Great booklet for beginners.

North American Butterfly Association (NABA). See write-up on NABA under "Learn From the Experts" heading to learn about extensive butterfly-watching opportunities with this national group.

Opler, Paul A., and George O. Krizek. 1984. *Butterflies East of the Great Plains: An Illustrated Natural History*. Baltimore: The Johns Hopkins University Press. This book is rich in natural history information; a must for your library if you live in or spend any time butterflying in the East. Covers 293 eastern species.

Pyle, Robert M. 1992. *Handbook for Butterfly Watchers*. Boston: Houghton Mifflin Company. A classic! A gem! A book that anyone interested in butterflies must have! This excellent introduction to butterfly watching is beautifully written and will educate newcomer and long-time butterfly enthusiast alike. Covers all aspects in a very readable way: watching versus catching, locating, identifying, record keeping, behavior, attracting (gardening for), raising from egg or discovered caterpillar, photographing, conserving, and understanding butterflies.

IDENTIFICATION

Glassberg, Jeffrey. 1993. *Butterflies Through Binoculars: A Field and Finding Guide to Butterflies in the Boston-New York-Washington Region*. New York: Oxford University Press. Covers the nearly 160 species found in the Northeast and teaches identification through the use of photographs of living butterflies in their natural poses and in the correct size relationship to other similar-looking species. Includes descriptions of selected butterfly hotspots and checklists for each. This book revolutionized butterfly watching by making identification of butterflies far easier than had most preceding field guides. Clearly a book for butterfly watchers, rather than collectors.

Glassberg, Jeffrey. 1999. *Butterflies Through Binocu-*

lars: *The East*. New York: Oxford University Press. Covers the more than 300 species found in the East and teaches identification through the use of photographs of living butterflies in their natural poses and in the correct size relationship to other similar-looking species. Includes color range maps which clearly show seasonality and number of broods. *Butterflies Through Binoculars: The West* (due out in 2001) will be another important tool. These publications and others in the series (focused on limited geographic areas: Florida, southern California, etc.) that will be coming out in the next few years are a *must have*. They, like their predecessor *Butterflies Through Binoculars: A Field and Finding Guide to Butterflies in the Boston-New York-Washington Region*, are sure to make butterfly identification possible for all. Armed with these guides, butterfly watchers across the country are sure to contribute greatly to the overall knowledge of status and distribution of butterflies.

Opler, Paul A. 1998. *A Field Guide to Eastern Butterflies*. Boston: Houghton Mifflin Company. In the renowned Peterson Field Guide Series. This latest production vastly upgrades all previous editions. Excellent and exacting range maps, conveniently located within the text, make it easy to see which butterflies might be found where you live or where you are traveling. Covers 524 eastern species. Illustrated in color with paintings of butterflies by Vichai Malikul that are complemented by 100 color photographs of live butterflies in natural settings. A modern classic. Another *must have*.

Opler, Paul A. 1999. *A Field Guide to Western Butterflies*. Boston: Houghton Mifflin Company. In the renowned Peterson Field Guide Series. This latest production has been long awaited by all westerners and those who travel in the West. Another *must have*.

Pyle, Robert M. 1981. *The Audubon Society Field Guide to North American Butterflies*. New York: Alfred Knopf. This book is illustrated with photos of live butterflies in natural settings (the first butterfly field guide to do so), as well as photos of a number of their eggs and caterpillars. It in-

cludes excellent natural history information and is the only true field guide (usable in the field for identification) to all of North America's butterflies north of Mexico.

Scott, James A. 1986. *The Butterflies of North America: A Natural History and Field Guide*. Stanford, Calif.: Stanford University Press. This weighty book is not for the field, but is an excellent reference manual. Be aware that the names used in this book predate accepted English names established by NABA. Continent-wide range maps graphically illustrate where butterflies are found. Covers 679 North American species. Illustrated with color photos of museum specimens.

Walton, Richard K. *Skippers of the Northeast: A Video Guide to Field Identification* (a 48-minute video). Richard Walton, 7 Concord Greene #8, Concord, MA 01742. Covers 45 species, including the males and females of many species. Focuses on field identification, but also shares examples of fascinating skipper behavior.

Wright, Amy Bartlett. 1993. *Peterson First Guide to Caterpillars of North America*. Boston: Houghton Mifflin Company. A wonderful addition to your library, devoted entirely to the identification of caterpillars of our most common butterflies and moths. This popularized book will, we hope, lead to a greater appreciation for the early life stage of butterflies and moths.

A SAMPLING OF REGIONAL BUTTERFLY BOOKS

Acorn, John. 1993. *The Butterflies of Alberta*. Edmonton, Alberta: Lone Pine Publishing. Illustrated with color photos of live butterflies. Range maps, informational species accounts.

Allen, Thomas J. 1997. *The Butterflies of West Virginia and Their Caterpillars*. Pittsburgh: University of Pittsburgh Press. A wonderful resource for all; will be especially useful for those who have struggled to identify unknown caterpillars. Many books describe the caterpillar stage, but this book illustrates them all with photos of caterpillars in natural settings (many of which have never before appeared in print). West Virginia range maps, county by county.

Bailowitz, Richard A., and James P. Brock. 1991. *Butterflies of Southeastern Arizona*. Tucson: Sonoran Arthropod Studies, Inc. A thorough review of the biology and the systematics of the butterflies of southeastern Arizona, including excellent regional information about each species (larval foodplant when known, flight period, distribution). Illustrated largely with black and white photos of museum specimens; to be used in conjunction with a field guide if intending to identify butterflies.

Brown, John, Herman Real, and David Faulkner. 1992. *Butterflies of Baja California*. Beverly Hills: Lepidoptera Research Foundation. Baja California range maps. Illustrated with photos of museum specimens. For each species includes peninsular distribution, flight period, and host plants.

Emmel, Thomas C., and John F. Emmel. 1973. *The Butterflies of Southern California* (Science Series 26). Los Angeles: Natural History Museum of Los Angeles County. Illustrated with photos of museum specimens; includes great drawings of caterpillars.

Emmel, Thomas C., Marc Minno, and Boyce Drummond. 1992. *Florissant Butterflies: A Guide to the Fossil and Present-Day Species of Central Colorado*. Stanford, Calif.: Stanford University Press. Fascinating information; illustrated with photos of museum specimens and some photos of live butterflies.

Ferris, Clifford D., and F. Martin Brown, eds. 1981. *Butterflies of the Rocky Mountain States*. Norman: University of Oklahoma Press. An excellent regional guide.

Gochfeld, Michael, and Joanna Burger. 1997. *Butterflies of New Jersey: A Guide to Their Status, Distribution, Conservation, and Appreciation*. New Brunswick, New Jersey: Rutgers University Press. Details historic information for 134 species found in New Jersey and neighboring states (plus 11 species that were historically present but no longer occur). Not a field guide, but an excellent reference manual.

Heitzman, J. Richard, and Joan E. Heitzman. 1987. *Butterflies and Moths of Missouri*. Jefferson City, Missouri: Missouri Department of Conservation. Illustrated with photos of museum specimens.

Holmes, Anthony M., Ronald Tasker, Quimby Hess, and Alan Hanks. 1991. *The Ontario Butterfly Atlas*. Toronto Entomologists' Association, 34 Seaton Drive, Aurora, Ontario L4G 2K1. Not a field guide, but a locator guide including maps (for each of the 148 species), annotated with dots showing where each has been found in Ontario's counties and districts. Very few plates; not all species illustrated.

Iftner, David C., John A. Shuey, and John V. Calhoun. 1992. *Butterflies and Skippers of Ohio*. Ohio Biological Survey Bulletin New Series. Vol. 9, No. 1. Thought to be one of the best regional works for the Midwest. A definitive work.

Klassen, P., A. R. Westwood, W. B. Preston, and W. B. McKillop. 1989. *The Butterflies of Manitoba*. Winnipeg: Manitoba Museum of Man and Nature. Color photos of life-size museum specimens, usually depicting males and females and upper and lower surface.

Minno, Marc, and Thomas Emmel. 1993. *Butterflies of the Florida Keys*. Gainesville, Fla.: Scientific Publishers. Covers 106 recorded species of the Florida Keys with color photos of museum specimens, including both upper and lower wing surfaces, and both sexes when dissimilar. Excellent natural history information.

Shull, Ernest M. 1987. *The Butterflies of Indiana*. Indianapolis: Academy of Science. Illustrated with good-quality color photos of museum specimens, showing variation within each species in color, size, and markings. This book was very educational in our formative years, helping us to understand that an individual might not look exactly like the picture in the book.

Tveten, John, and Gloria Tveten. 1996. *Butterflies of Houston & Southeast Texas*. Austin: University of Texas Press. Covers more than 100 species of butterflies found in southeastern Texas. Illustrated with photos of live butterflies in natural settings; includes photos of the caterpillars of many species. The life history information is very useful, much of it new to many readers.

Monarch Information

Brower, Lincoln P. 1995. "Understanding and mis-understanding the migration of the Monarch butterfly (Nymphalidae) in North America: 1857–1995." *Journal of the Lepidopterists' Society*, Vol. 49, No. 4: 304–385.

Grace, Eric S. 1997. *The World of the Monarch Butterfly*. San Francisco: Sierra Club Books. A beautifully written, up-to-date review of what is known about Monarchs.

Herberman, Ethan. 1990. *The Great Butterfly Hunt, the Mystery of the Migrating Monarchs*. New York: Simon and Schuster. A children's book about the search for the Monarch's winter roosts in Mexico. Excellent source of facts about the quest and the discovery.

Lasky, Kathryn. 1993. *Monarchs*. New York: Harcourt Brace & Company. A children's book about the Monarch's life cycle, incredible migration, and winter roost sites in Mexico. Excellent source of solid factual information about something very complicated.

Urquhart, Fred A. 1998. *The Monarch Butterfly: International Traveler*. Ellison Bay, Wisconsin: Wm. Caxton Publishers. An updated version of Urquhart's original book, *The Monarch Butterfly* (published in 1960 by the University of Toronto Press), which has long been out of print and unavailable. It is written for a more general audience.

Butterfly Gardening

Ajilvsgi, Geyata. 1990. *Butterfly Gardening for the South*. Dallas: Taylor Publishing Company. Full of fascinating natural history information. An excellent book on butterfly gardening; useful to all gardeners, not just those in the South.

Brooklyn Botanic Garden. 1995. *Butterfly Gardens: Luring Nature's Loveliest Pollinators to Your Yard*. Brooklyn: Brooklyn Botanic Garden.

Buchmann, Stephen L., and Gary Paul Nabham. 1996. *The Forgotten Pollinators*. Covelo, Calif.: Island Press. Excellent natural history information about butterflies and other forgotten pollinators and the role they play.

Dennis, John, and Mathew Tekulsky. 1991. *How to Attract Hummingbirds & Butterflies*. San Ramon, Calif.: Ortho Books.

Dole, Claire Hayen, ed. *Butterfly Gardeners' Quarterly*. P.O. Box 30931, Seattle, WA 98103. Four issues profile plants, butterflies, garden styles, people, organizations, and events related to butterfly gardening.

Ernst, Ruth Shaw. 1996. *The Naturalist's Garden: How to Garden with Plants That Attract Birds, Butterflies, and Other Wildlife*. Old Saybrook, Conn.: The Globe Pequot Press.

North American Butterfly Association (NABA). See write-up on NABA under "Learn From the Experts" heading to learn about NABA's publications, all of which include articles about or focus on butterfly gardening (*American Butterflies, Butterfly Garden News*, introductory butterfly gardening brochures, and more than twenty-one regional butterfly gardening brochures).

Stein, Sara. 1993. *Noah's Garden: Restoring the Ecology of Our Own Back Yards*. Boston: Houghton Mifflin Company. Addresses America's landscape style of neat yards and gardens that have devastated suburban ecology. Stein's next book, *Planting Noah's Garden, Further Adventures in Backyard Ecology* (Houghton Mifflin Company, 1997), explores how many have tried to undo damage done by traditional landscape practices and restore their backyard ecosystems. Both books are inspirational and practical.

Stokes, Donald, Lillian Stokes, and Ernest Williams. 1991. *The Butterfly Book: An Easy Guide to Butterfly Gardening, Identification, and Behavior*. Boston: Little Brown & Company.

Tekulsky, Matthew. 1985. *The Butterfly Garden: Turning Your Garden, Window Box or Backyard into a Beautiful Home for Butterflies*. Boston: Harvard Common Press.

Tufts, Craig, and Peter Loewer. 1995. *Gardening for Wildlife: How to Create a Beautiful Backyard Habitat for Birds, Butterflies and Other Wildlife*. Emmaus, Pa.: Rodale Press.

Xerces Society / Smithsonian Institution. 1990. *Butterfly Gardening*. San Francisco: Sierra Club Books.

VIDEOS

A number of videos on butterflies and gardening for butterflies are available and sold in many nature centers. Some people find videos to be useful learning tools.

RECORD KEEPING

LepiList is IBM-compatible software for recording sightings. It contains the NABA species list, lets you keep this list up to date, and lets you add nearly 10,000 other Lepidoptera. Available from Santa Barbara Software Products, Inc., 1400 Dover Road, Santa Barbara, CA 93103; Phone: 805-963-4886.

MacFritillary is Mac software for recording sightings. It contains the NABA species list, allows for full listing and reporting, and has an auto life list, easy notebook-style entry, and instant species accounts. Available from Whole Life Systems, 20 Parsons Street, Kennebunk, ME 04043.

North American Butterfly Association (NABA). 1995. *NABA Checklist & English Names of North American Butterflies* (1st Edition). Morristown, N.J.: NABA. This publication includes the 717 species of butterflies that have been recorded in North America north of Mexico. It standardizes English names of North American butterflies and has made the study of butterflies far less frustrating. Most field guides that have been published since this checklist have adopted these standardized English names. Novice butterfliers will now be able to spend more time learning and less time sorting out which butterfly is which.

LEARN FROM THE EXPERTS

The British Butterfly Conservation Society, P.O. Box 222, Dedham, Colchester, Essex C07 6EY Great Britain. Phone: (01206) 322342, Fax: (01206) 322739, E-mail: butterfly@cix.compulink.co.uk. A nonprofit British organization (formed in 1968) dedicated to saving wild butterflies and their habitats by creating nature reserves; advising landowners; carrying out research, surveys, and monitoring; lobbying, educating, and campaigning; and reestablishing species as part of planned species recovery programs. *Butterfly Conservation News*, their official journal, is published quarterly. As of 1997 this group had 30 branches, run entirely by volunteers.

Cape May Bird Observatory (CMBO), Center for Research and Education, 600 Route 47 North, Cape May Court House, NJ 08210; Phone: 609-861-0700. World Wide Web site: www.nj.com/audubon. CMBO's Cape May Birding Hotline (609-861-0466), updated each Thursday evening, includes noteworthy butterfly sightings and natural history information. CMBO's "Birding and Butterflying Map to Cape May County" features public butterfly gardens and natural areas that are hotspots for butterfly (and bird) watching. CMBO's "Checklist of Butterflies of Cape May County, New Jersey" is updated regularly and reflects the region's unique butterfly fauna, noting seasonality, status (how common, uncommon, etc.), and migratory species. CMBO offers butterfly walks each spring and fall, butterfly identification and gardening workshops, tours of private butterfly gardens, and has published literature on creating habitat for birds, butterflies, and dragonflies. CMBO's two centers have bookstores with complete sections on butterfly identification and gardening. A model backyard habitat at CMBO's Center for Research and Education features butterfly and hummingbird gardens, wildflower meadows, and more. CMBO's Northwood Center in Cape May Point features butterfly and hummingbird gardens and habitat. CMBO's Monarch Monitoring Project conducts Monarch surveys and wing-tagging (3,000–7,500 Monarchs tagged) at Cape May each fall.

Friends of the Monarchs, P.O. Box 51683, Pacific Grove, CA 93950; Phone: 408-375-0982. Pacific Grove is a seaside community on the Monterey peninsula famous for sheltering overwintering Monarchs October through March. A 1939 city ordinance authorizes a $1,000 fine for "molesting a butterfly in any way." Contact Friends of the Monarchs for more information about Pacific Grove's Monarch sanctuary and protection efforts.

Journey North, 125 North First Street, Minneapolis, MN 55401; Phone: 612-339-6959. World Wide Web site: www.learner.org/jnorth/. Journey North is a global study of wildlife migration (including Monarchs) for schools.

The Lepidopterists' Society, 1900 John Street, Manhattan Beach, CA 90266. An international organization of amateurs and professionals dedicated to the study of butterflies and moths. Established in 1947.

Monarch Program is devoted to Monarch conservation and publishes a monthly newsletter *(The Monarch Newsletter)* from October through May. Monarch Program, P.O. Box 178671, San Diego, CA 92177 or E-mail to: monarchprg@aol.com. Established in 1990 as an educational public benefit organization with the objective of preserving Monarch breeding and overwintering habitats, monitoring migration of western Monarch populations, and working on educational materials and conservation issues.

Monarch Watch, a nonprofit organization founded in 1992, is dedicated to education, conservation, and research. Monarch Watch is a collaborative network of students, teachers, volunteers, and researchers investigating the Monarch butterfly migration phenomenon and its biology. The program seeks to involve thousands of students and adults by sending out butterfly tagging kits, a newsletter, and maintaining a World Wide Web site with many opportunities. Monarch Watch, c/o Orley R. Taylor, Department of Entomology, University of Kansas, Lawrence, KS 66045; Phone: 785-864-4441. E-mail to monarch@ukans.edu. World Wide Web site: www.MonarchWatch.org. Postings on Monarch Watch's Web site include some of the easiest-to-understand and most up-to-date explanations of very complicated topics: Monarch migration, overwintering sites, conservation, life cycle, and lots more. Also included

are details of tagging, mapped tag returns, and other research programs. Monarch Watch participants tagged 50,000 Monarchs in the fall of 1997.

North American Butterfly Association (NABA), 4 Delaware Road, Morristown, NJ 07960; Phone: 973-285-0907; 800-503-2290 (membership inquiries only). World Wide Web site: www.naba.org. A national group for anyone interested in butterflies. NABA is a nonprofit organization that was formed in 1992 to promote nonconsumptive, recreational butterflying and to increase the public's enjoyment, knowledge, and conservation of butterflies. NABA produces a number of publications. *American Butterflies* is NABA's quarterly journal and includes articles on butterfly identification, photography, hotspots, gardening, and conservation issues. *Butterfly Garden News* is NABA's quarterly newsletter and includes articles on all aspects of gardening for and attracting butterflies by authors from around the country. NABA's Program for Butterfly Gardens and Habitats has produced a set of introductory butterfly gardening brochures that are applicable throughout the United States and Canada as well as 21 regional butterfly gardening brochures (as of January 1998). To purchase these or for up-to-date information on which regions are covered by a regional brochure, contact NABA Butterfly Gardens and Habitats, 909 Birch Street, Baraboo, WI 53913. NABA also has local chapter meetings and field trips. For up-to-date information on local NABA chapters, contact NABA, 4 Delaware Road, Morristown, NJ 07960. NABA holds biennial members' meetings around the country: 1994 in southern New Jersey; 1996 in Sierra Vista, Arizona; and 1998 in Golden, Colorado. NABA also organizes and publishes the results of more than 300 4th of July Butterfly Counts across North America and in Mexico. These counts were started in 1975 and have been held annually since. They were sponsored by the Xerces Society for the first 18 years and then transferred to NABA's sponsorship in 1993. NABA is also responsible for standardizing the English names for all 717 species of butterflies recorded in North America north of Mexico, and has produced *The North American Butterfly Association (NABA) Checklist & English Names of North American Butterflies* (first edition 1995), available for sale from NABA.

Southeastern Arizona Bird Observatory (SABO), P.O. Box 5521, Bisbee, AZ 85603-5521; Phone: 520-432-1388. World Wide Web site: www.sabo.org. SABO offers activities featuring the birds, butterflies, and other wildlife of southeastern Arizona, including spring and summer walks at local natural areas and workshops on wildlife-friendly gardening. The popular Living Jewels workshop in August highlights the wildflowers that follow the summer rains and the butterflies, hummingbirds, and other pollinators they attract. SABO also offers information about local natural areas, wildlife viewing opportunities, trip planning, and more for visiting nature enthusiasts.

The Xerces Society, 4828 Southeast Hawthorne Boulevard, Portland, OR 97215; Phone: 503-232-6639. The Xerces Society is an international nonprofit organization dedicated to the global protection of habitats for butterflies and other invertebrates.

TRAVEL AND BUTTERFLY-WATCHING TOURS

American Birding Association Sales (ABA), P.O. Box 6599, Colorado Springs, CO 80934. Phone: 800-634-7736. *ABA Sales Annotated Catalog and Price List* offers, by mail-order, a complete list of regional birding guides (arranged by state for the United States, by province for Canada, and by country for the rest of the world).

Butterflies Through Binoculars Tours, Inc., 4 Delaware Road, Morristown, NJ 07960; Phone: 973-285-0890. Butterfly-watching tours to parts of the country where diversity is high; tours led by Jeffrey Glassberg, author of *Butterflies Through Binoculars*. Tour destinations have included the overwintering sites for Monarchs in Mexico, the Lower Rio Grande Valley in Texas, Florida and the Keys, California, southeastern Arizona, Colorado, New Jersey, and other sites.

Dr. William Calvert, 503 East Mary Street, Austin, TX 78704; E-mail: wcalvert@bga.com. **Texas Monarch Watch**, Phone: 800-468-9719. Dr. Calvert offers customized trips to see the Monarch overwintering colonies. These tours also focus on Mexico's endemic birds, anthropology, and culture.

Victor Emanuel Nature Tours (VENT), P.O. Box 33008, Austin, TX 78764; Phone: 800-328-VENT or 512-328-5221; Fax: 512-328-2919; E-mail: VENTBIRD@aol.com. VENT offers customized trips to see the Monarch overwintering colonies as an extension of one of their other trips.

BUTTERFLY FESTIVALS

North American Butterfly Association, Dr. Gary Ross, Director of Butterfly Festivals, 6095 Stratford Avenue, Baton Rouge, LA 70808. The popularity of butterfly festivals is growing; Dr. Gary Ross is interacting with groups that are either planning for or thinking about hosting a butterfly festival.

Mt. Magazine International Butterfly Festival, c/o North Logan County Chamber of Commerce, 301 West Walnut, Paris, AR 72855; Phone: 800-980-8660; Fax: 501-963-8321. Usually held in early August.

Texas Tropics Nature Festival, P.O. Box 790, McAllen, TX 78505; Phone: 800-250-2591. Some years this festival includes butterfly tours, native plant tours, and butterfly-gardening seminars. Usually held in late April.

Index

How to Spot Butterflies

How to Spot Butterflies

About the Authors

PATRICIA TAYLOR SUTTON is the program director and naturalist at New Jersey Audubon Society's Cape May Bird Observatory. Formerly she was senior naturalist at Cape May Point State Park. In these positions, she has taught thousands about the wonders of birds, botany, and bugs — particularly butterflies. She is the editor and coauthor of New Jersey Audubon Society's publication *Backyard Habitat for Birds, Butterflies, and Dragonflies: A Guide for Landowners and Communities*, and has written extensively on how to create butterfly and hummingbird gardens.

Clay Sutton is a freelance writer, lecturer, wildlife biologist, naturalist, and bird tour leader. He is coauthor with Pete Dunne and David Sibley of *Hawks in Flight* and of *North American Birds of Prey* (National Audubon Society Pocket Guide) with Richard Walton. As a former environmental consultant specializing in endangered species, he conducted many surveys for rare and threatened butterflies.

Pat and Clay are coauthors of two previous guides in the How to Spot series: *How to Spot an Owl* and *How to Spot Hawks and Eagles*. They are founding members of the North American Butterfly Association (NABA) and Pat is on NABA's board of directors.

The Suttons live near Cape May, New Jersey, a location known primarily for its bird migration, but which is equally spectacular for its autumn butterfly migration of Monarchs, Common Buckeyes, Red Admirals, and others.